THE STOP
MATT MALOUF
DOING LIST

THE
STOP
MATT
MALOUF
DOING
LIST

MORE TIME
MORE PROFIT
MORE FREEDOM

WILEY

First published in 2017 by John Wiley & Sons Australia, Ltd
42 McDougall St, Milton Qld 4064
Office also in Melbourne

Typeset in 11.5/14.5 pt Palatino LT Std

© Envisage Australia Pty Ltd 2017

The moral rights of the author have been asserted

National Library of Australia Cataloguing-in-Publication data:

Creator:	Malouf, Matt, author.
Title:	The Stop Doing List: more time, more profit, more freedom/Matt Malouf.
ISBN:	9780730337447 (pbk.)
	9780730337454 (ebook)
Notes:	Includes index.
Subjects:	Success in business.
	Creative ability in business.
	Business enterprises—Australia.

Cover design by Kathy Davis/Wiley

Printed in Singapore by C.O.S. Printers Pte Ltd

10 9 8 7 6 5 4 3 2 1

Disclaimer
The material in this publication is of the nature of general comment only, and does not represent professional advice. It is not intended to provide specific guidance for particular circumstances and it should not be relied on as the basis for any decision to take action or not take action on any matter which it covers. Readers should obtain professional advice where appropriate, before making any such decision. To the maximum extent permitted by law, the author and publisher disclaim all responsibility and liability to any person, arising directly or indirectly from any person taking or not taking action based on the information in this publication.

CONTENTS

ABOUT THE AUTHOR

Matt Malouf is a passionate business coach, speaker, author and entrepreneur on a mission to help entrepreneurs around the world break the shackles of mediocrity and reach new levels of personal and business success.

Looking Back

Matt launched his career as an Ernst & Young accountant after graduating from Sydney University in Accounting & Finance. He has since enjoyed a varied career that has seen him work with start-up ventures, right through to some of Australia's largest companies including Rio Tinto, AMP and Aon Hewitt.

This experience enables Matt to teach entrepreneurs how to apply big business principles in a small business environment to fast track growth.

Having started, grown and sold a number of businesses himself in a variety of industries, Matt also has hands on experience with every stage of the business lifecycle, from conception through to exit strategy.

Approach to Coaching

Matt's business coaching methodology is simple. First, you need a strong understanding of where you are *now*, including all the variables that are restricting and supporting your business growth.

Once you're clear on your current coordinates, Matt begins mapping the journey from where you are now, to where you want to be. He works with you to establish meaningful, measurable and achievable goals by which to track your progress, keeping you accountable and ensuring you're always moving in the right direction—with pace.

With a winning combination of traditional and contemporary business education and the support of structured accountability calls, Matt helps clients uncover what their businesses need to shift from ordinary to extraordinary by becoming the facilitator of change.

Proven Results

A multipotentialite drawing knowledge and experience from a host of industries and personal mentors, Matt has helped clients add millions of dollars in turnover, with most doubling or tripling profitability in under 12 months—all without pressure on internal resources.

His eye for recognising lucrative opportunities, matched with proven strategies, gives his clients a competitive edge in every aspect of business. While a focus on 'quick-wins' is central to success, it is the accountability element that helps Matt's clients turn visionary ideas and bold plans into profitable results.

Areas of Expertise

With extensive training in every area of business including sales, marketing, leadership, human resources, strategy and finance, Matt takes a holistic approach to uncovering the roadblocks in your business and uses a hybrid of tools to creatively overcome challenges by implementing systems and continually improving processes.

Whether yours is a startup or an established business, Matt refines every detail from the ground up, ensuring your business is both efficient and profitable.

Looking Forward

A balanced and mindful husband, father and entrepreneur himself, Matt's goal is to help fellow business owners worldwide achieve business fulfilment faster than they ever dreamt possible—without sacrificing personal relationships or recreation.

To achieve this, he has developed a system that helps business owners excel in their own 'personal mastery', teaching new-age strategies for becoming more disciplined and better time managed.

Matt helps business owners understand and focus on what they need to 'stop doing' as opposed to the traditional methods of time management that focus on to-do lists and calendar management.

ACKNOWLEDGEMENTS

I want to thank all of the amazing business owners who have inspired me to write this book. This book would not exist without your commitment and dedication to growth.

To Andrew Jones—your help and guidance through the process of putting the book together was amazing. Without your help this book would not exist. Thanks for listening and somehow understanding what I was trying to get across—you're a legend mate!

I would like to thank my mum and dad—Roger and Margaret Malouf. Your never ending support and belief in me inspires me to be my best every day and I thank you for all that you do for me and my family.

Lastly to my wonderful wife Danielle and our three children—Aden, Scarlett and Avalon. You guys are the greatest joy in my life and the Stop Doing List system was ultimately created so I could spend more of my life with you—so thank you for your patience, belief and love.

FOREWORD BY SIIMON REYNOLDS

Every year, millions of people decide to take a giant leap toward their dreams and open a business.

At first it's exciting. But for too many entrepreneurs, the feelings of euphoria soon get replaced with frustration, as they get overloaded with hundreds of tasks they feel they must do just to keep their business afloat.

It's not unusual for the entrepreneurial dream to then become a logistical nightmare. The To Do List becomes bigger, the hours become longer and the happiness becomes smaller and smaller until, in many cases, it gets snuffed out entirely.

That leads to a phenomenon that is all too common—the Zombie Business.

A company is a Zombie Business when it is barely alive and is being run by an exhausted, unmotivated entrepreneur who no longer even likes their business, yet is forced to stay in it, out of financial necessity or just because of a dogged determination not to give up on it. It's the corporate equivalent of the walking dead.

The tragedy of the Zombie Business is not just that there are thousands of them, it's the fact that it never had to be this way.

If their owners had known the right things to do and correct ways to think, they could have built a vibrantly thriving business that delivered on the promise and hope of its original founding: to provide a wonderful, growing income while affording the business owner a balanced, joy-filled lifestyle.

But all is not lost. You have in your hands a tactical sword that can slay the Zombie and get you back on track to creating the business that you deep down have always dreamt of.

This is not the usual business book, no siree. This teaches a radical way of thinking and acting that is the complete opposite of current business norms.

Matt Malouf is an evangelist for a totally different type of business—one that puts the happiness of the owner first and foremost. One that produces mountains of money without valleys of mental stress. One that enables you to use your time so well that you achieve far more than you ever have before, and yet paradoxically have more leisure time, not less.

Of course, the book world is full of authors proffering the secret to this and that, promising complete business and life transformation for 20 bucks. Why should you believe that Matt Malouf actually knows what he's talking about?

His experience, for one. Matt has built not one, but several successful businesses from scratch. No mean feat.

He is also one of the most eminent business coaches in the world, helping literally hundreds of entrepreneurs each year build both a better business and a better life.

The Stop Doing List features some of the advanced, highly effective strategies that other business owners have paid thousands of dollars to learn in Matt's courses, and yet are yours for a fraction of that price. What a bargain.

If you yearn to own a company that creates serious wealth without taking over the rest of your life, you are going to need to do things very differently from the typical business owner. This book truly shows you how.

Reading *The Stop Doing List* should be right at the top of your Start Doing List.

Siimon Reynolds,
Best-selling author of
Why People Fail

INTRODUCTION

If you're like most business owners I work with, you probably got into business to earn more money, have more time and find more freedom. However, many business owners feel like they've lost control of their business and life.

Rather than earning more money, they're making less than they did when employed—and are often losing money in the bad years. If they have an employee or two, often they're paying them more than they pay themselves.

Rather than having more time, they're working longer hours, up to 70 or 80 a week, sacrificing a social life, their health and even family to keep their business running.

Rather than having more freedom, they find themselves tied down to the business, unable to take a day off, let alone a holiday, for fear their business will suffer.

Rather than the growing, healthy business they dreamed of having, they're stuck in a business suffering from:

- low profit (or even losing money)
- no growth
- stagnation.

Meanwhile, as business owners, they:

- can't exit their business
- suffer from burnout
- have health problems arising from stress.

Since entering the world of business coaching and consulting, I've come across these problems time and time again with my clients. As I watched them transform their businesses through doing *less* work every day, I was inspired to write this book.

The Stop Doing List is not about giving you more work to do; rather, it's about identifying low-value tasks in your day-to-day routine, then stopping them. I've watched businesses rocket from stagnation to year-to-year growth through implementing these simple practices.

Through this book you will:

- get a clear assessment of your own value as a business owner
- find a way to start decluttering your business
- learn to implement a step-by-step Stop Doing List system in your business.

Your Stop Doing List involves more than just delegating or outsourcing; it starts with your mindset. Far too often the restrictions in businesses come from the owners themselves. Part I goes in depth into the fears surrounding delegation—and how those mindsets can be changed.

Then in part II we move into the Stop Doing List, a simple step-by-step system of working out what to stop doing. As you go through this system, you'll learn how to:

- focus on the activities that truly generate the profit in your business
- identify background tasks that simply distract you
- only do the tasks you love, allowing you to love your business.

Finally, in part III we set out the nuts and bolts of how you manage your people and your business effectively with a less-is-more approach, and how you actually find people for your team.

The last thing I wanted to do was give you yet another book dealing only with theory, telling you what you should be doing but not *how* to implement the solutions. So please take the time to complete the exercises and answer the questions throughout the book. When you commit to the work you will achieve amazing results. I have also created a step-by-step guide to make it really easy to implement the Stop Doing List system, downloadable from www.stopdoing.com.au.

I hope the Stop Doing List helps you find what you dreamt of when starting your business: freedom, increased profit and the time to spend on what is truly important to you.

PART I
YOUR
MINDSET

It's said that Einstein defined insanity as doing the same thing over and over again and expecting a different result. If this is true, then most business owners are insane. They turn up day after day to do the same job the same way, yet they hope to get improved results.

Business owners often fall into the trap of working too deeply *in* their business rather than working *on* their business, believing this is the only way they can maximise profit. Beyond that, many business owners play out a different form of insanity, in which they try *different* things with the *same* mindset, and expect a different result.

This mindset often creates frustration when business owners spend their time, day in and day out, doing the same low-value tasks. It almost becomes the culture of the business—incredibly difficult to break or replace with the mindset of growth, which always looks for a better way of doing business.

Mindset's an important starting point because, when it comes to our business, our behaviour is driven by our emotion. Unless we adopt the right mindsets and have a different attitude and outlook, then we'll only play out insanity.

No business can change overnight. Often it requires a series of small steps, beginning with the owner changing their mindset and implementing changes to the way they work. Correct mindsets, when multiplied by effective actions, equal amazing results. Once this process is started, businesses start seeing growth, little by little, bit by bit.

Correct Mindsets × Effective Actions = Amazing Results

CHAPTER 1
GET INTO THE LEARNING ZONE

Do you like to control every aspect of your business? While you may answer yes to this question, I am here to tell you that doing everything does not give you more control. If anything it reduces your ability to control your company, as you are spread so thin that things slip through the cracks. So you decide you need to let go and you try to delegate some tasks. You employ someone or outsource some tasks to someone, only for them to screw it up—*again*—so you are left to clean up the mess, and the little voice in your head says, 'I *told* you it would be easier to do it yourself.'

You see, in order for the Stop Doing List system to work for you (and it does work), you need to understand it's not as simple as telling somebody what to do. For the system to succeed you must be committed to behavioural change.

In order to achieve a goal you have never achieved before, you must start doing things you have never done before. This behavioural change is required for you and your people, but inevitably it must start with you! This sounds easy, but if it were that easy there would be no need for this book. Behavioural change requires you to consistently do something different.

Without understanding that you must leave your comfort zone in order to achieve behavioural change, you will struggle to let go of the majority of the non–income generating tasks that are holding you and your company back. Figure 1.1 shows the different zones.

Figure 1.1: the comfort, learning and panic zones

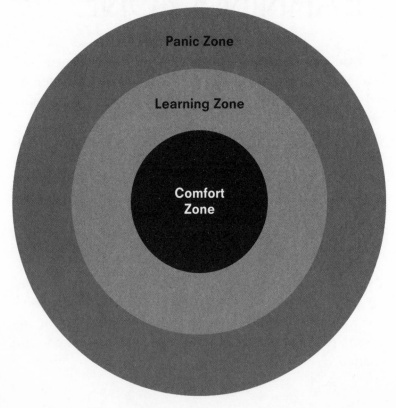

The comfort zone

We have all heard the term 'comfort zone' used in business in some way or another. It is where many business owners operate from. Put simply, it's where our natural skills and abilities lie. For many business owners, their comfort zone is filled with big lists of what they need to do, which tend to be lower value tasks that have high urgency. When I first start working with a business owner their comfort zone rarely consists of focusing on tasks that will move them towards their goals faster.

It is important to note that if you choose to spend the majority (if not all) of your time in the comfort zone you will make little progress, if any. This is because your comfort zone consists of things you can already do quite easily. You are unable to learn and build new skills in the comfort zone.

The panic zone

Quite often the people I work with make a decision to jump out of their comfort zone to move towards their goals. This is often after reading a book, attending a seminar or hearing someone inspiring that fires them up. Their challenge is they jump so far out of their comfort zone that they become stressed, anxious and even overwhelmed, which often leads to inactivity (the opposite of what they are trying to achieve!). We refer to this as the panic zone. When you are in the panic zone every activity or task feels tough and unachieveable. You will find yourself in a state of confusion or panic and feeling so uncomfortable that achieving the tasks is near impossible.

Like the comfort zone, you can't make progress from the panic zone. I find a lot of business owners enter the panic zone when they take on too many new tasks or projects. Your goals and dreams will not be realised from the panic zone.

The learning zone

The learning zone is the zone between the comfort zone and the panic zone. This is where real progress is made. The learning zone is where new skills are learned and mastered. It is where you will gather forward momentum towards your goals and often see great revenue and profit improvements in your business.

To be honest, while the learning zone is the more appropriate name for this zone, I personally like to call it the 'earning' zone. In the earning zone you will feel a little uncomfortable. This is good: growth cannot occur in your comfort zone. The easiest way to explain this is a simple metaphor. If you have ever trained with weights in the gym you will understand that if you choose:

- easy weights to lift you will make no progress
- weights that are too heavy you will more than likely injure yourself
- weights that challenge you to the point where you can safely do 10 repetitions and physically cannot push another one out, you will achieve growth.

This is the learning zone.

Identifying the learning zone

Many business owners don't know where their comfort zone ends and their learning zone begins. Because progress can only be achieved by performing tasks within the learning zone, we must first define the boundaries of this zone. 'So how do I know which zone I am in?' you may ask.

Well let's start with your comfort zone. If you don't find yourself challenged and rely largely on habit or past experience, chances are you are working inside your comfort zone. Start to take note of the tasks you naturally choose to do, or tasks that don't stress you out. Please note that you don't want to avoid performing tasks in your comfort zone; in fact, at times it may be beneficial to the business. But you want to avoid spending *all* of your time in the comfort zone.

On the opposite end, the panic zone is quite easy to identify. Tasks or activities in the panic zone often create high levels of stress, do not come naturally to you, and are often short-lived because of the amount of 'pain' they create for you. An example of the panic zone is adults learning to swim. Often the student is stressed and unsure, causing their body to tense right up. This stressed state makes it impossible for them to learn and often causes them to struggle and be unable to stay above the water. It's only when the student begins to relax and understand how to get their body to float that they can begin to learn how to swim.

So, if we know that in the comfort zone things appear to be predictable or too easy, and the panic zone is characterised by high stress or feeling frantic, the learning zone is easier to define. This growth zone is where we perform optimally and begin to enjoy tasks, putting us in a prime physical and emotional state for both absorbing and retaining information—not too stressed, not too relaxed. Now I'm not saying that it's going to be easy! You will feel a little stretched at times and even bordering on the panic zone. But in my personal experience (and the experience of my clients) the learning zone will return you 10 times your effort if you are persistent. Being able to recognise which zone you are operating in and understanding the physical and emotional corrections required to reach the learning zone results in ongoing progress and personal development.

Get comfortable feeling uncomfortable

With the zones continually morphing it can be difficult to remain within the learning zone. You therefore need to embrace being uncomfortable, knowing you are primed for progress in this state.

When you take on new and challenging tasks, you will notice with repetition they become familiar, transitioning you from the learning zone to the comfort zone. Similarly, tasks once tackled in the panic zone will become more manageable and descend into the learning zone, and so the process continues.

Implementing the Stop Doing List system might send you into the panic zone if you try and stop everything all at once. You will repeat old behaviours and thought patterns that will cause you to think 'It's easier if I just keep doing this' or 'I'll never be able to find someone who can do this as well as I can.'

In order to prevent this from happening, we want to start slow. The Stop Doing List system is designed to assist you to take a step back into the learning zone and do some preparation, research or documentation. This process develops new skills and abilities, which move you from the panic zone into the learning zone, and ultimately (by making regular, conscious efforts) into the comfort zone.

You've got to understand you have to do things differently; you have to let go. You can allow people to perform many of the tasks on your to-do list, make mistakes—just like you did when you learnt the first time—and your business will not end! Otherwise, you'll be doing these tasks forever. You'll be experiencing the same challenges and you'll never move forward.

However, while this all sounds quite easy, it will require behavioural change to become reality. The ultimate blocker to you letting go will be fear. Fear of:

- failure
- people making mistakes
- losing control.

The list goes on. Yet fear is not real. It is all in our imagination. Take skydiving as an example—for some people this is the most terrifying act they can think of, while for others it is the most exciting and exhilarating rush of their lives. The only difference between these two conclusions is the belief system of the individual. One of the ways to break through your fears is to run at them as hard and fast as you can.

Commit to learning a better way, a different way. Commit not only to starting the change, but also to mastering the change and making it your new reality.

CHAPTER 2
FOUR NEGATIVE MINDSETS TO RESET

Being a business owner in today's ever-changing business landscape is a tough game. The pressure and constant stress can wear many of us down—and that little voice in your head may not be doing you any favours. This little voice has more control than you think and is one of the major drivers of success or failure. What holds many business owners back from delegating or outsourcing tasks is the story that little voice is constantly repeating.

Through my work as a business coach and asking my clients 'what holds you back from delegating many of the tasks on your to-do list?', it became apparent that there were four negative mindsets that kept coming up:

1. They can't do it as well as I can.

2. I don't want to give up control of the task.

3. I can't afford it.

4. I don't have the time to implement this.

These mindsets need to be understood and eliminated in order for you to effectively implement the Stop Doing List system.

Negative Mindset 1: 'They can't do it as well as I can.'

This is the lamest excuse I have ever heard, and one of the most common! You need to understand that most of what you do is not unique and that many of these tasks can be done by others. It's certainly a big obstacle to overcome—trying to come to a place of accepting that someone else can't do it as well as you can. And the truth is, on some tasks, that is actually true. I am not recommending that you stop doing the tasks that you are brilliant at and make you money; I'm saying you should stop doing the tasks that have to be done, but are of low value to your business.

These low-value tasks have a tendency to fill our days, pushing us away from those tasks we are brilliant at. Even if you are brilliant at the low-value tasks, your energies are better spent on the task that is going to make you the most profit.

So why can't they do it as well as you can? It is my observation that many business owners do not set people up to 'win'. In order to enable someone to do a low-value task as well as you can (or better), you must:

- *Clearly explain what you expect from them.* Set a clear expectation of the deliverable, time frame, work standard, and so on. Do not leave it unspoken.

- *Train the person how you want it done.* This is often done by having a clearly documented system and spending time with the person, allowing them to understand how you want the task done.

- *Have a system for accountability and reporting in place.* This will enable you to oversee the task being done without having to do the doing. All of this is covered in detail in part III.

Many times when a team member doesn't do a good job at a task, it's because of one or two reasons:

1. *The person isn't the right fit for the task or for your business.* This is where defining your culture and how team members fit in (covered in chapter 11) is important. You also need to spend time matching the person and their strengths to the right tasks. For example, someone whose strength is sales is often very people-oriented and is often a terrible fit for an administrative role that requires someone to be very task- and detail-oriented.

2. *They haven't been taught well.* This is often the major reason team members fail, especially when the business owner is only just starting out with a team. Training someone in a role is more than just walking them through the steps a few times. Everyone learns differently, and being able to adapt your training to suit someone's learning style is extremely important (this is covered further in chapter 8).

The key to training your people is to teach them how you think when you are performing the task. Teaching the step-by-step sequence is not enough. Remember that you have been performing this task for a long time and probably feel as if you perform it automatically. But the reality is you're asking and answering a series of questions in your head every time you perform the task—you just haven't taken the time to teach this to others.

Negative Mindset 2: 'I don't want to give up control of this task.'

The next excuse I'll often hear is, 'I don't want to give up control of this task.' For many people, their business is like their child. They care for it, nurture it and slave over it, spending years of blood, sweat and tears on it. They would do anything for that child. But a business matures just like children do. In time you have to allow it to function without you holding its hand. If you don't, if you control it too tightly, the business will not be allowed to grow.

There's a concept from the Hubbard Management System called the knowledge–responsibility–control (KRC) model (discussed further in chapter 7). Knowledge, responsibility and control work as a combined force. To achieve the desired results in any area of life, it is crucial to have a degree of knowledge about it, to assume some responsibility for it and to take control of it.

Many tasks cannot be delegated because the business owner is the only one with the necessary knowledge. There is no documented system, and it's time-consuming to train people, so it seems easier for you, as the business owner, to just do it. Now, if increased knowledge is the path to responsibility and control, then as long as you remain the most knowledgeable, guess who remains responsible for and in control of the task? That would be you!

In order to let go of control of a task, it's essential you focus on educating someone within your team to perform it. As you increase their knowledge, you empower them to take more responsibility, which in turn allows them to take control of the task or situation, ultimately removing it from your own to-do list. It's often a business owner's inability to teach effectively that is the missing ingredient.

You need to find the right balance of control versus freedom for your team so they can make their own choices as your business matures. Business owners who tightly control all areas of their business often inadvertently stifle growth. When you begin to let go of control, the business almost takes on a life of its own. When teams are empowered to make decisions independently the business often grows exponentially without the business owner having to work harder.

It's perfectly natural to have a higher level of control when your business is young. During the start-up phase of most businesses, the owner is required to be very hands-on due to limited resources. But having the mindset and systems ready to take advantage of the Stop Doing List system as the business matures will see the business grow faster.

Negative Mindset 3: 'I can't afford it.'

'You *really* can't afford it?' is often my response when a business owner tells me they can't afford to hire someone to help them. Time is your most precious commodity. It is nonrenewable, and how you choose to invest your time will ultimately determine your success or failure. Most business owners dismiss the idea of getting help, without exploring all of the options available to them.

In order to conclude you can't afford help, you need to be clear how you are making this assessment. Many business owners simply look at the hourly rate of the person they would delegate the task to and conclude 'I can't afford it.' This is a very narrow-minded view, and certainly not what I would call an entrepreneurial view. In order to calculate the cost–benefit analysis of getting help, first you need to know your hourly rate. (This is covered in chapter 6.) Then assess how much time the chosen task will take to perform, and extrapolate this over 12 months to obtain a per annum cost.

Let me give you a quick example.

TASK: UPDATE DATABASE RECORDS DAILY

Time to complete task	=	6 minutes per day × 5 days per week (30 minutes per week)
Hourly rate of current owner of the task	=	$75 per hour
Current owner cost to complete the task per week	=	$37.50 per week
Current owner cost to complete the task per year	=	$1950 per year

Let's assume that this task is delegated to an offshore assistant and their hourly rate is $10 per hour.

Offshore assistant cost to complete the task per week	=	$5 per week
Offshore assistant cost to complete the task per year	=	$260 per year
Net gain	=	$1690 per year

Now it's important to understand that there is also an opportunity cost here. If you were to invest the 30 minutes per week you now save into an income-producing activity, the opportunity cost of you choosing to do the low-value task is double the calculated gain. This is because in choosing to perform the lower-value task you forgo the opportunity to complete an income-producing task. So, using the previous example, instead of making you $75 per hour, updating the database records actually *costs* you $75 per hour. The benefit, then, of outsourcing the task is 2 × $1690 = $3380 per year.

Let me give you a simple example that I see regularly. Take business owners who spend several hours a week doing the books, when a bookkeeper can do it often in half the time and to a higher standard. Despite this, many business owners will still insist on doing it themselves, in order to save a little bit of money. This is a clear example of a task that should not be done by a business owner and should be outsourced or delegated to a specialist. In this example, it's entirely possible that it's costing the business owner more (in money and time) by doing it themselves, with higher accounting fees down the track—not to mention the hours lost that could be spent on higher-value tasks or a personal life. And let's not forget the increased stress and frustration of doing something they may not be particularly good at!

Meanwhile, employing a bookkeeper to come in and do your books will save you a lot of heartache and time, as they already know the best way to work with your accountant's preferred bookkeeping system. They move through bookkeeping tasks at the higher efficiency that comes from working in their 'genius' every day. You get several hours of your week back, time you could spend on profit-generating tasks or with your family and friends or pursuing hobbies. You'll end up with a set of books that reduces the time your accountant needs to spend preparing your tax returns. You might actually come out ahead just on the fees you save with your accountant.

In today's globalised market, there is always an affordable option available. Internationally, there is a massive pool of low-cost, high-value talent available for hire. For example, virtual assistants from the Philippines have excellent English, and many have already practised many of the skills you're looking for. Often these options are very affordable. Now, having taught this material for many years, I know you may have some negative thoughts around using overseas options. I'm often asked, 'How can you sleep at night knowing how little you pay these people?' The reality is, I personally pay all of my overseas people the rates they ask for. So while this may seem low to us, to the people setting the fee it's great money. It is, in my opinion, a real win–win.

Even locally there are untapped pools of workers. As an example, take parents looking to get back into the workforce; they may only want to work a day or two a week, and only a few hours a day, to fit in around their children's school time. Or workers who are close to retirement age, who want to stay in the workforce in a part-time or contracting capacity and who bring with them a wealth of skills and experience, not to mention a great work ethic. Some of the best workers you might ever find are people from these pools, due to their life experience and flexible work options.

Whether it's a local or international team member, or role-based or task-based outsourcing, there's always an inexpensive option to help you get to your goals. Remember, unless your skills are developed to an expert level, it's quite possible that there's someone out there who can do the work in a fraction of the time you take to complete it, so it may not even be as expensive as you expect.

Negative Mindset 4: 'This is all good, Matt, but I just don't have time to implement this.'

Wrong, wrong, wrong! If you hear yourself saying the words 'I don't have the time', then reading this book has become a thousand times more important. If you're serious about being successful in your business, then you *must* make the time to implement this system. Your business (and life, for that matter) will never move forward if you continue to adopt the same behaviours and self-talk.

The biggest killer of implementation is being busy in the day-to-day of running and operating your business. Being busy doesn't make you more money. Being busy doesn't serve your customers or clients better. Being busy doesn't make your life better. The aim is to stop being busy and start focusing on what you love to do and what makes you more money. I can guarantee you will be grateful you did and wonder why you wasted so much time. So start stopping now!

EXERCISE
1. List the negative mindsets that you adopt regularly.
2. What impact are these mindsets having on your business and your life?
3. What do you believe this is costing you in lost profits?

CHAPTER 3
FIVE ESSENTIAL MINDSETS TO GET

There is no doubt in my mind that adopting the correct mindset is essential to succeeding in business, and in life, for that matter. A Tony Robbins quote sticks in my mind: 'Success leaves clues and so does failure.' The five essential mindsets discussed in this chapter have been modeled on successful entrepreneurs who have applied the Stop Doing List system and grown amazing businesses.

These mindsets are learnable and require focus and discipline to master. They are not a 'tick the box' exercise, either—they are fundamental to your continued growth and success and need to be applied and lived daily.

Essential Mindset 1: Say no

Success is often found when we say yes to opportunities without too much thought, knowing we will work out the 'how' later. This reflex is often a result of our desire to prove ourselves and before we know it we're saying yes to opportunities even if they seem frightening. We may also say yes to avoid missing out or out of the fear that declining an opportunity may send the wrong message to the people asking.

However, success tends to breed success and before you know it greater opportunities start coming your way. It then becomes critically important and a challenge to prioritise the many opportunities on offer, which often leads to not definitively saying no in an effort to keep our options open. This, as you might expect, leads to a lack of clarity as we take on more than we can handle, and we end up letting people down, burning out and inevitably failing. To avoid this scenario we need to get into the habit of confidently and respectfully saying no, making it clear that we are choosing not to pursue this specific opportunity, while at the same time preserving a strong relationship for future opportunities. The foundations required to build this skill come from how we manage our emotions when making the decision.

The emotions I'm referring to here may seem insignificant: a slight feeling of regret, elevated stress, the voice in your head saying 'Do you really want to say "no" to this?' To avoid feeling such emotions, we often say 'yes' and gain some reprieve. While this decision offers some short term pain relief it will not serve you in the long term. Remember, we will do more to avoid pain than we will to achieve pleasure. A critical step in managing these emotions then, is to remind yourself that by saying no today you will reap greater rewards in the future.

It is critical to your success, and to regaining control of your time, that you learn to say no. For many of us the learned behaviour started as a child, as many of us were brought up to NOT say no. No was considered a bad word and we were often punished for saying no, rather than taught the value of saying no at the right time.

While many people say yes to please another person to avoid feeling negative emotions, in many cases this leads to failure. If you say yes and can't follow through—not because you don't want to or intend to but simply because you don't have the time to do everything you have said yes to—then you inevitably let the person you said yes to down. This is, in many cases, worse than saying no in the first place.

Many business owners stunt their business growth by not saying no. They refuse to say no to clients asking for more than they're paying for; they don't say no to tasks that take them away from building their business and, even more importantly, that take them away from their family. Saying no is an integral part of the Stop Doing List system. It's a skill that we have to learn and, like any skill, it takes practice to get it right and time to learn how to do it.

To achieve success in business it is essential that a business owner be accountable for all of their commitments (whether they are answering yes or no). This must be coupled with managing the expectations of others. While this may sound simple it can be quite challenging to implement. Here are five tips to help you say no with more confidence:

1. *Back-of-the-envelope pros and cons.* Making a decision with information in front of you is always easier. By simply writing down the pros and cons of either a yes or no decision enables you to clearly see the implications of your decision.

2. *Actions speak louder than words.* It is important that your actions are consistent with your words. If you are constantly answering yes to things and not following through because you really should have said no, then you will find yourself with more challenges than if you simply said no in the first place. Set yourself some clear rules and boundaries and stick to them.

3. *If you're not 100 per cent committed to your answer, then ask for time.* Often we are so busy that we are not 100 per cent present when saying yes or no. If you are unsure whether to answer yes or no to a request then it is reasonable to ask for some time to finalise your decision. You might use this time to check your schedule or chat with your team before committing to an outcome.

4. *Calculate the ROI.* You must start to associate a real cost to everything you do. Your time is worth money and you need to ensure you are investing it for maximum return each day. When presented with an opportunity, simply calculate the hours you expect the task or project to take and multiply

this by your hourly rate (which we calculate in chapter 6). This simple back-of-the-envelope calculation will make the decision easy.

5. *Share your reason for saying no.* Many of the people you start saying no to may not be used to this answer from you. They may feel rejected and this may strain the relationship. By simply sharing your reason for saying no (you simply have too much on, can't free up enough budget at the moment, etc.) you will generally get a more positive response and maintain strong working relationships.

Learning to say no in the right way will accelerate your success and is a must if you are to successfully implement the Stop Doing List System. It will take a little time to build your confidence and consistency, but stay with it—it will pay you dividends in the long run.

Essential Mindset 2: Less is more

There's a common misconception among business owners and entrepreneurs that by doing more work they become more successful. I don't know where they learnt this—when you look at successful businesspeople, the opposite is most often the case.

Analyse what you do every day. If you're like most business owners, the majority of your work produces little income, if any, and doesn't need to be done by you. If you instead focus on the tasks with the highest return and spend increasing amounts of time on those tasks, you will make more money.

Most business owners end up majoring in minor tasks that have minimal or zero financial or emotional return to them or their business. I'm not saying these tasks don't need to be done; what I am saying is that these tasks don't need to be done by *you*. This is the starting point of the Stop Doing List system.

When you don't have to do these low-value tasks yourself, you start reclaiming your time rather than trying to fit everything in by working more hours. If you start to measure the amount of time you spend in your genius (that is, the highest-yielding tasks) and spend more time on these tasks, you should see a direct increase in your revenue and profit.

Work hard on the *right* tasks, the most productive and highest-returning tasks, to get results. Don't fall into the trap of equating success with having the biggest to-do list: less is more.

Let me share a quick example. I worked with a client named Adam who owned a mid-size building and construction company. Adam's primary role was sales and marketing, while his business partner took care of project management. When I first met Adam he was doing everything. He was doing the sales, the marketing, the admin, the quoting, the invoicing, and so on. He was working over 70 hours per week and did not have a life outside of work.

One day I called him and asked him what he was up to. He told me he'd just returned from a networking event and was entering the details of the half-dozen business cards he had collected into their customer relationship management (CRM) system.

'You're *what*!?' I said. This was a simple and clear example of a task a business owner should stop doing. Adam had invested his time into meeting new people and connecting with them, but why should he be the one to enter them into the CRM? Adam's response was typical of most entrepreneurs I meet: 'If I don't do it nobody will, and I can't afford to hire anyone else at the moment.'

The best return on Adam's time was in having meetings with prospective clients and winning their work. The more meetings Adam had with the right people, the more opportunities he'd find, the more proposals he'd send out and the more sales he'd complete.

While this seems logical, it is often challenging for business owners to implement because of the negative mindsets discussed in chapter 2.

I helped Adam identify all of the tasks he was performing at less than his calculated hourly rate and assisted him in hiring a part-time virtual assistant in the Philippines named Sebastian. Sebastian's hourly rate was $7.

Now after Adam attends a networking event, he takes photos of the business cards and gets Sebastian to import all the information into the CRM. Sebastian also triggers an automated thank-you email, including a link to book a meeting with Adam, to the new contacts.

Fast-forward 12 months and Adam had doubled the size of his business. He was able to cut his workload by 20 per cent and focus more time on the income-producing tasks. Sebastian was working full time (35 hours per week) and continued to support Adam and his business in their continued growth.

This is just one example of how less is more in business. By adopting a less-is-more mindset, Adam was able to identify the tasks with the biggest return, then stop doing everything else so he could focus his time on growing the business.

Essential Mindset 3: Investment, not expense

It should be no surprise to anyone reading this that in taking the next step with your business, there will be costs. But it is how you view these costs that will determine whether your business progresses (and to be honest it will more than likely go backwards than stay where it is).

When considering the costs there are two common, but very different, mindsets you can adopt.

An expense mindset

An expense mindset means viewing every dollar spent as a cost and having a very short-term view. Often the first thought when asked to make a decision is 'I can't afford that' without considering the future benefits in spending that money. An expense mindset will limit your inner growth, and hold you back from achieving your full potential.

If you choose to view the money spent on delegation and outsourcing tasks or functions as an expense, what you are really saying is you aren't expecting a return on the money. As with rent or phone bills, there's not really any *direct* return on the money; rather, it's an expense incurred in the running of the business. Through this lens you will almost always choose to delay implementing the Stop Doing List system and inevitably slow your business growth.

An investment mindset

When you view decisions as investments and not as expenses or costs, you open yourself and your business up to a whole new world of possibilities. Often business owners who adopt an investment mindset have clarity about their goals. They have written plans and are strategically growing their business, rather than letting their fears hold them back.

With an investment mindset, when you choose to delegate a task or outsource a function, you will be focused on bringing on the right person. You will view the wage or salary you are paying as an investment, because you will understand that the time you save will enable you to focus on higher-income-earning tasks. To put it simply, if I invest in an employee salary of $40000 a year, and it then frees up my time to generate an extra $150000 of profit for the business, I'm $110000 ahead.

Believing that when you engage a new team member you are making an investment rather than incurring an expense will open you and your business up to a whole new world of possibility.

The starting point to work out your return on investment is to understand your hourly rate. You need to have something to measure your return against. (We go into how to calculate your hourly rate in chapter 6.)

In order for a business owner to achieve the mindset of viewing delegation as an investment rather than an expense they simply have to make a decision. It really is that easy! However, this simple decision often comes with a lot of resistance and struggle as a result of the business owner's fear and uncertainty. To switch from an expense mindset to an investment mindset, consider the following:

- Business owners simply don't have enough time to do everything.

- Delegation of low-value tasks will create a positive return on investment in the long run.

- The more time a business owner spends generating profit, the more successful the business will be.

- The longer the right team member remains part of the team and receives training in their tasks, the greater the return on investment.

Now, there are no guarantees. There's no guarantee that the first person you hire will be the right person. In fact it is highly likely that they won't be. You might select the wrong person for the role, or fail to train them to do the job as well as you can. It's all part of the process of learning how to Stop Doing.

But following the Stop Doing List system will ensure you prevent many of the common mistakes along the way and will fast track you to success.

Hopefully throughout this process you'll come to understand that without people (either local or overseas) you'll never grow your business in a significant and sustainable way. You can choose to stay as a solo entrepreneur, in which case all you've really done is bought yourself a job. The true definition of a business is a commercial profitable enterprise that can operate *without* you.

Essential Mindset 4: The 80/20 principle

After reading *The 80/20 Principle* by Richard Koch and putting his theories into practice, I soon realised that this counterintuitive approach was critical to business success. *The 80/20 Principle* states:

> that a minority of causes, inputs or effort usually leads to a majority of the results, outputs or rewards. Taken literally, this means that, for example, 80 per cent of your results come from 20 per cent of your efforts (and conversely the other 20 per cent of results come from the other 80 per cent of efforts).

When applying the rule to you and your business, if you focus on the 20 per cent of effort that produces 80 per cent of the result, then your team can focus on the 80 per cent effort required to complete the task or project. If you apply this consistently across everything you do then effectively you've increased your productivity by 500 per cent.

This rule is transferable across every part of your business, and life in general. You should check it out; in any given situation, you'll often find the rule in effect. If you were to break down your annual revenue, you should find that close to 80 per cent of your sales belong to only 20 per cent of your clientele. Even here, it suggests where you should focus the majority of your energy and time. Rather than spreading yourself thin around your whole client base, if you focus your attention on these high-value clients (and prospects) you'll get the best result. Delegate managing and servicing the bottom 80 per cent of clients to people who can do the job 80 per cent as well as you can.

Identifying the 20 per cent of tasks that will get you the 80 per cent of results comes back to identifying your genius, which is covered in chapter 5. When you identify the top three to five tasks you love to do, you're exceptionally good at, and are the highest earning tasks in your business, you can turn around and eliminate practically everything else—because 80 per cent of your business results actually come from your efforts in those genius areas.

The 80/20 rule is even applicable a second time around. If you've already worked out 80 per cent of your revenue comes from the top 20 per cent of customers, you can then take the rule and apply it again. What you will often find is that 64 per cent of the revenue actually comes from the top 20 per cent of the top 20 per cent of customers.

To put this in numbers, if you had $100000 of revenue and 100 clients, you'd get $80000 of revenue from only 20 clients. When you apply the rule again, you'd discover that $64000 actually comes from only four clients.

Take a look at all tasks that need to be done in your business and apply the rule to them. What tasks on the list have little impact on the bottom line? You'll probably find around 80 per cent of tasks fall into this category. If you were to stop doing those tasks, handing them over to someone else, your time would be freed up for the important 20 per cent of tasks that will grow your business. Once you've completed that process, you can repeat the calculation to focus your time on the 4 per cent of tasks that get you 64 per cent of your bottom line results. You can let systems and well-trained team members look after the rest.

Essential Mindset 5: Don't sweat the small stuff

At this point, any savvy business owner should be doing a risk assessment on the possible impact of applying the Stop Doing List system. The risks should be weighed up and compared to the benefits of delegating low-value tasks and focusing on your genius.

In his book *The One Thing to Win at the Game of Business*, Creel Price talks about three different levels of decision making. Price teaches that it is essential that we don't see all decisions as equal. He also states that it is important for entrepreneurs to understand that it is not essential to get 100 per cent of their decisions right. To quote Price, 'You don't have to be right all the time to create a very successful business'—and I couldn't agree more! Put simply, all of the decisions you make as a business owner can be put into three categories: minor, major and mega decisions.

Minor decisions

Minor decisions are the day-to-day decisions that all business owners are required to make (such as the decision to purchase a new printer). Price suggests that your minor decisions only need to be right 25 per cent of the time or more for your business to be successful. The challenge as I see it is most business owners are majoring in minor decisions: they are spending too much time on these minor decisions or not allowing others to make these decisions.

Major decisions

Major decisions are larger decisions that tend to cost a bit of time and maybe money. Price suggests your major decisions need to be right 50 per cent of the time or more to have a successful business. Major decisions often make a big difference in the long run, while not being huge, life-changing ones. They may take a little time and thought, but you can usually bounce back from a wrong choice quite quickly and easily. These decisions are ones business owners need to practise making efficiently, learning from any mistakes made, and moving forward to the next decision.

Mega decisions

A mega decision is a big business-critical decision, and these need to be right 75 per cent of the time or more. These can be questions such as 'Should we purchase the premises for the business?', 'Should we bring in an investor?', or 'Who do we hire as a managing director?' If you can get a majority of these decisions right, generally speaking you will have a very successful business. These will often be decisions where you spend a significant amount of time researching and weighing up the options. If you get them wrong, they tend to be the ones with the greatest negative impact.

Worst-case scenario

The decision of whether to apply the Stop Doing List system sits somewhere between the minor and major level of decision. It may cost some time and money, however it shouldn't be agonised over for long. The reality is many of the tasks you need to stop doing have minimal negative impacts on the revenue and profitability of your business in the long term. They're just tasks that need to get done.

Continuing the example of bookkeeping from earlier, that's a decision that falls into the major level. It may cost some time and money to get the systems right, and time to research and find the right bookkeeper. However, many business owners treat this as a mega decision instead, and procrastinate on it, preferring to do the books themselves. Often they'll stay up late trying to balance the reconciliation rather than finding someone who can deliver far better results, faster. You can see the decision to get a bookkeeper is really quite a minor decision in comparison to others you may need to make.

As you assess and manage the risks of delegation, look at the worst-case scenario. What if your team member makes a major mistake? What is the exposure of the business? Is it time? If so, how much time? Is it money? If so, how much money? How much hit to your reputation would there be if there was a mistake? If you start with the worst-case scenario, it actually shows you how much time you need to spend slowing down, building the right system, training your staff, and working with them to ensure it's going to get done right every time.

***

Adopting these essential mindsets is critical to your success. Study them, apply them and understand that they are a *must*. The right strategy with the wrong mindset will always fail. Ultimately, you want to be confident when you implement the Stop Doing List system. What's more, with the right preparation and mindset, your confidence won't need to be faked.

We are now moving on to the 'how to' of the Stop Doing List system. Please be sure to continuously refer back to part I if you are stuck, because 99 times out of 100 the answers to your struggles are within this section—not the how to!

EXERCISE

1. How confident (out of 10) are you when it comes to saying no? (1 = lowest, 10 = highest)
2. Create a list of tasks you perform regularly that you know you need to stop.
3. List circumstances where you find yourself saying yes but wishing you said no. What emotions would you feel if you said no in these circumstances?
4. List 'minor' decisions you tend to procrastinate on.
   (a) What stops you from making a quicker decision?
   (b) Describe the worst-case scenario for you and your business if you make a wrong decision.

PART II
CREATE YOUR STOP DOING LIST

Creating a Stop Doing List sounds quite simple: write a list of the things you want to stop doing. There, done! However, of course it is not that easy.

The Stop Doing List system is a five-step system to help you clearly identify what you need to stop doing and whether you are ready to stop doing the task or activity:

1. Complete a time log.
2. Calculate your hourly rate.
3. Identify your genius.
4. Filter tasks through the Focus Funnel.
5. Write your Stop Doing List.

Before I step you through the system there are some foundational concepts to understand that will fast-track the application of the system. These concepts include:

- *Your time is worth money.* Have a clear understanding of what your time is worth in dollar terms, and learn how to maximise your return.

- *Discovering your Genius Zone.* In this zone you only do the tasks or activities you love, you are really good at, and that have a great financial return for you and the business.

CHAPTER 4
YOUR TIME IS WORTH MONEY!

Time is irreplaceable. If you lose money, you can always make more; waste your time, and you'll never get it back. All of us have a limited number of seconds in our lives. We don't know how much time we really have, yet we don't treat it with enough respect.

This is even truer in business. Every second spent in your business is time spent building something to help people, generate profit and build a future for you and your family. So when you spend your time on tasks that don't build your vision, it becomes lost time. Having a clear value on your time is key to the success of the Stop Doing List system.

The busyness trap

When we spend so much time working in our business, often our perspective gets warped and shifted out of proportion. Urgent work tasks are often mistaken for important ones. We get caught in the trap, taking on these urgent tasks, getting them done, and receiving the emotional reward of 'well done, you've completed a task,' and we remain in that cycle day in, day out.

When you work for an employer, you have the advantage of someone managing your time. Not only are you told what to do (and, often, how to do it), you are given deadlines and time frames, often working with other people who have to meet their own deadlines.

More than that, you are told what your time is worth by your employer. Your hourly rate is set by the government, agreement or contract, and you always know what an hour is worth to you (and to your employer). Whether you are working for $15 an hour flipping burgers or $100 an hour managing a company, your hourly rate is usually clear (if not, your weekly, monthly or annual rate certainly is). You know how much effort is required to earn that hourly rate, and if you want to keep earning, you need to work hard at the tasks set by the boss. You know that if you waste an hour while working you might suffer penalties, and so are kept accountable.

Along the way, as we became business owners, many of us lost track of knowing the value of our time. We started looking at the list of tasks we had to complete rather than understanding what tasks or roles were essential to complete to maximise our hourly return as the business owner. Often we sacrifice our time on tasks that, however necessary they are, add nothing to the bottom line. We start treating all tasks as equal and, instead of guarding our time as our most precious commodity and carefully choosing where we will spend it, we waste it.

This all starts when we begin our business. We have limited money to invest yet we believe we have an endless amount of time. Without someone to delegate to, we take all tasks on ourselves, further diluting our hourly rate with work that doesn't actually add money to our pocket.

To further damage the value of our time, we often don't pay ourselves a wage that actually reflects what we put into the business. Despite putting 50, 60 or 70 hours a week into our businesses, we pay ourselves last, out of what's left over after paying everyone else. Employees are often far better paid than many business owners, for far fewer hours, and they handle a much lighter workload. This can breed resentment towards our employees, and make us long for the days when our work lives were dictated to us by our employer. Days when we got to go home with money in our pocket, and without staying back to put in unrewarded overtime.

No-one's going to value our time for us. Not our customers, not the government, not our accountant (although maybe a good one will talk to you about it). No-one will tell you that you need to set your price higher (especially not your clients).

I also believe that, if you don't value your time properly, it will be reflected in how you work and communicate with your clients and customers. When you feel like you are being underpaid, or even at times like you are working for nothing, then you naturally will not be your best for your customers. When you respect and value your time, your clients will too and they will inevitably be willing to pay you more also.

When you don't value your time, you'll just end up working, working, working, allowing other people to put their agendas ahead of yours. Whether it's a client, a business partner or a supplier, everyone is out to ensure their agenda gets prioritised. Time and priority management are necessary to ensure your time doesn't get consumed and your agenda doesn't get pushed to the side.

On a personal level, when you don't value your time your work ends up eating away at your life. We don't live to work; we work to live. As much as many of us love what we do (myself included), our businesses are there to serve us and the people we care most about. Yet many business owners get into business only to find they end up spending less time with the people who matter, less time on things they love, and instead spend all their time working. It becomes their entire life.

It doesn't have to stay that way. As a business owner, you have control over your mindset and how you implement decisions in your life. You can make a change right now in your business, without consulting a boss or manager. If you want to restructure your business to place an emphasis on the value of your time, you can make that decision and just do it.

Time management

Let me share a classic time management story with you. A professor has a jar sitting on her desk. Large rocks fill it to the top. The professor asks the class if the jar is full. To which they reply, 'Yes, of course it is.' The professor then takes a handful of pebbles from behind her desk. When she drops them into the jar they settle in around the rocks. She then asks the class, 'Is the jar full now?' To which they respond, 'Okay, okay—now it's full.'

The professor now pulls out a cup of sand and pours it into the jar. The sand fills in comfortably around both the rocks and the pebbles. The professor asks once more if the jar is full. Now realising that it couldn't possibly be filled with anything further because there is no visible space the students say, 'Okay, now it's definitely full.'

From behind her desk the professor pulls out another element: a jug of water. She pours it in, filling the last remaining space in the jar. She turns to the class and says, 'In life, we often think we can do no more. But when we are creative we find that there is always room for us to fill.'

This story is probably one of the oldest in the personal development world, and it's the perfect illustration of how time management is usually viewed. It's the efficiency argument: there is almost always a way to fit more in. If you develop the tools and techniques to manage your time efficiently, you can maximise the number of tasks done in a single day.

The Stop Doing List system runs counter to this. Trying to fit more in is not the way to grow your company and will inevitably lead to mistakes, reduced growth and burnout.

The real weakness of the 'rocks, pebbles, sand' analogy is that it doesn't allow for an important part of reality. In the demonstration everything fits nicely into the jar if you organise it the right way and put in the elements in the appropriate order. But in the real world you can be perfectly organised and still run out of capacity—not to mention that the goal is not necessarily to fit more in. Remember, the goal is simply to produce more positive results.

But to use the same mentality, let's suppose that the jar represents the 24 hours in your day, and it's filled with water. You've reached absolute maximum efficiency in every single thing you did during the day—there's no room in the jar for air, let alone rocks, sand or pebbles. What you would eventually find is that, no matter how well you managed your time and no matter how efficiently you worked, the jar of your day would eventually overflow.

Why? Because there is more to do than you can ever do. There is always something else you could do. There are always more improvements you can make. There is something that you can add. There is some other place that you can go—and on and on and on.

This is not to say that efficiency isn't still very much worth incorporating into our lives. But because there is always more to do than you ever can do, the efficiency paradigm eventually caps out; its benefit is limited.

Here is the truth: you can't really manage time. Everyone talks about time management skills. You may have even picked up this book because you think you have room for improvement or you're curious about time management strategies. Well, sorry to disappoint you, but there is no such thing as 'time management', at least not in the way that it is popularly conceived. There is only self management. You can't manage time. You can't control time. You can't start or stop time. You can work fast or slow but time carries on at the exact same rate regardless of what you do.

You can, however, manage yourself. You can decide which things are worth investing yourself in and which are not. You can choose to either be focused on things that matter or to allow yourself to be swept away in a sea of distraction. And once you grasp this truth you are ready to implement the Stop Doing List system.

Genius tasks and valuing your time

When you spend more time on your genius tasks (more about them in chapter 5), your business will start to experience amazing growth. This is the core of the Stop Doing List. A genius task is described as a task that has a great financial return, that you love to do and that you are really good at. These are the 'rocks' in the jar described earlier and need to be prioritised. Everything that is not a genius task can be done by someone else.

Business owners will start seeing growth in their business once they get into their genius tasks, such as:

- working on sales
- creating marketing

- developing new products
- designing business systems
- motivating and inspiring their team.

Many businesses I've worked with who have followed this system are doubling, tripling and even growing at 500 per cent or more as they implement what I'm teaching. The profit is not in doing minor, lower-value tasks, but in doing the high-value tasks, and focusing time and energy on them.

Every day you put off the decision to change how you value your time is another day full of precious seconds wasted on low-value tasks easily performed by other people. Focus your time on the activities, people and hobbies you love.

Find a system that works

Over the past 30 years or so it seems there has been a lot more focus on prioritising, largely thanks to *The Seven Habits of Highly Effective People* by the late, great Dr Stephen Covey. Dr Covey's simple time management matrix, as shown in table 4.1, which measures urgency against importance, allows us to sort tasks into four different quadrants:

1. Urgent and important
2. Not urgent and important
3. Urgent and not important
4. Not urgent and not important.

Table 4.1: time management matrix

	Urgent	Not urgent
Important	*Quadrant I* Urgent and important	*Quadrant II* Not urgent and important
Not important	*Quadrant III* Urgent and not important	*Quadrant IV* Not urgent and not important

- Quadrant I is for the items that need to be dealt with immediately.

- Quadrant II is for items that are important but do not require immediate attention.

- Quadrant III is for tasks that tend to suck up our time. These should be minimised or eliminated.

- Quadrant IV is for tasks that offer little to no value. These are typically trivial or time-wasting tasks used as a break from the urgent and important activities.

Dr Covey emphasised that results come by focusing on quadrant II: important but not urgent tasks. These are tasks such as planning your strategy, relationship building, and recognising and investing in new opportunities.

The challenge for most of us, though, is that we give up these quadrant II activities by allowing ourselves to be sucked into the quadrant I (important and urgent) activities.

When you compare business owners who are 'successful' to those who have 'failed', take a look at how they've spent their time. The successful business owners are far more selective with their time, almost guarding a resource they value as priceless. They become increasingly successful, while business owners who don't value their time try to do everything, and often end up failing.

While this isn't a time management book, we can't begin to implement the Stop Doing List without giving you some basic tools to use in your day-to-day routine so you can take advantage of the time you'll be freeing up.

It's important to understand that there isn't a single perfect way to manage your time. With various methods and systems you can use, it comes down to understanding what works for you and then implementing different systems until you find the right fit.

For example, you may use a written to-do list in a notebook, while other people choose to use an app, or their email system's task list. All of them are achieving the same outcome, but there isn't one perfect way to do it.

What you *must* understand is the underlying theory doesn't change from system to system; only tools vary. Time management needs to become a continuous study, something you constantly work on. I've personally tried various online systems, programs, apps, read many books, and implemented with paper and technology alike. It's working out the method, taking a little bit from each system and finding what works best for you. Given the underlying theory doesn't shift, the tools are relevant to the outcome as long as they help you achieve what you want to achieve.

I strongly recommend you become a student of time management. Once you've calculated your hourly rate, it should become apparent: any investment that can buy back your time is a worthwhile one. Every cent invested into learning how you can become more efficient with your time and increase your productivity will pay dividends in the long run.

Measurement is key

If you want to improve your time management, you must begin to measure where you are spending your time. Michael Gerber talked about this in *The E-Myth*, saying, 'We can't manage what we don't measure', along with the second part of the equation: 'What you measure improves.' Before you can assess what you should stop doing, you first must understand how you use your time, and where you're spending your time every day.

In order to start the Stop Doing List process it is essential that you measure where you are spending your time. I recommend keeping a time log for at least two weeks. This involves documenting—in 15-minute increments—how you are spending your time (from when you wake to when you go to sleep). You can use the time log tool in the Ultimate Stop Doing List Tool by simply going to www.stopdoing.com.au

Basically, what you're doing is documenting what you do from the moment you wake up through to the moment you go to sleep, logging your activities in 15 minute increments. This enables you to keep track of what's happening at a high level.

After the two weeks spent logging your time, you need to sit down and group your activities into categories, such as personal and business. From there, you break those down into even smaller categories; for instance, with business, you might break it down into:

- admin
- human resources
- finances

- legal
- sales and marketing
- customer service
- emails and phone calls
- time spent producing your product or service.

Personal categories can be broken down into:

- family
- social life
- relaxation
- hobbies
- movies, TV, games
- community contribution.

These categories help give you a detailed view of what you're spending your time on. You might find you're spending a large amount of time in areas of your business that are low value compared to tasks that contribute directly to your bottom line.

The best thing about measuring your time is the data doesn't lie. You could be really busy all day, convinced you're spending your time on valuable tasks and being really productive, but until you measure it you don't really know. Measuring it gives you facts you can use to inform your decisions going forward.

CHAPTER 5

DISCOVERING YOUR GENIUS ZONE

The ultimate goal of the Stop Doing List system is to help you spend more time in your Genius Zone. Your Genius Zone is the three to five major tasks you own in the business and that you invest the majority of your time into in order to generate maximum return. A genius task meets the following three criteria:

1. *It's something you're passionate about.* First and foremost, a genius task needs to be something you enjoy, something you love doing. Without that passion, you're not going to put in the time, energy and effort required to push your business to new heights.

2. *It's something that is essential to the business.* It must be done, even if nothing else is done all day. Your business hinges on this task being completed, and being done right.

3. *It needs to contribute directly to the profit of the business.* As you begin to value your time, it'll become increasingly important to you to spend your time on profitable tasks.

The four zones

I first learnt this method of categorising tasks from my studies of Dan Sullivan, founder of the Strategic Coach program and an international author, speaker and coach. I slightly altered his definitions as I began implementing the Stop Doing List system for myself and others. Please note that these are definitions to be applied to tasks or activities *only* and are by no means a definition of your intelligence or abilities.

Tasks fall into one of the following four zones, as shown in figure 5.1:

1. Incompetence

2. Competence

3. Excellence

4. Genius.

Figure 5.1: the four zones

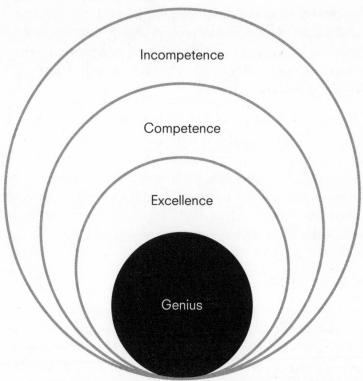

For most, the Genius Zone is where they *should* spend most of their time, as it's where most of the profit will be made. Yet most business owners I meet are often spending very little if any time in this zone.

The ultimate goal is to spend the majority of your time on 'genius' tasks, with a bit of time on 'excellence' tasks, and the rest of the tasks now become your Stop Doing List. When you stop doing these tasks, you'll find you are now focusing on areas that will ultimately provide more profit.

If you aren't good at a task, you delegate it to someone who can be excellent at it. Meanwhile you're freed up to spend more time on what you love doing, and you'll gain more passion for your business. You'll find more freedom in your business and find more time for family, health and personal passions.

I've been discussing genius a bit, and for good reason. When you begin to focus your time on your genius, not only do you start growing your business faster and generating more profit, but you also start enjoying business more. The tasks you choose to do every day contribute to your overall enjoyment when working, and the time being reclaimed will bring balance back into your life.

Incompetence

Tasks that are placed into the Incompetence Zone are tasks that you know have to be done, but don't know how to do them yourself. To give you an example, when we implemented a piece of software in our business called Time Trade, I received the link from someone else, did some quick research and saw it would be a great fit for our business. It could save us both time and money, but I had no idea how to implement it properly. It's simply not my genius.

I suggested the new system to my virtual assistant, and got her to research it, try it out and make a recommendation as to whether or not it was the right fit. It then became her responsibility to integrate it within the business, tying it in with our existing systems. I didn't need to know how to use it myself, other than telling clients how to book an appointment with me. (Which is pretty simple—click the link and book a time!) We then made sure the system was documented. This was all put in place by my virtual assistant, who is the one using it most of the time. Thanks to the documentation it can be picked up by anyone in our business in the event my virtual assistant is sick or leaves the company.

When we are learning anything new it often takes a long time and requires a lot of focused energy to implement. These tasks are often low value and create negative energy when you implement them (stress, angst, frustration).

The goal is for you to spend 0 per cent of your time performing incompetence tasks.

Competence

Tasks placed into the Competence Zone are tasks you know how to do but are not very good at or loathe doing. These tasks really drain you of energy. For most business owners this is admin, filing, bookkeeping, or many of the current technology needs a business has, such as social media, search engine optimisation or Google AdWords. These are tasks you can do, but you really shouldn't. Not only will it take longer for you to do it than someone operating in their genius, but it will also often add to your overall lack of satisfaction in your business.

In my work with clients I see a lot of tasks deemed 'urgent' falling within the competence category. There is inevitably a long list of these tasks and business owners tend to procrastinate or avoid doing them, which causes them to build up and create even more stress. Many of these tasks can be performed by someone else for a fraction of your hourly rate.

Again, the goal is for you to spend 0 per cent of your time doing competence tasks.

Excellence

Tasks that are placed into the Excellence Zone are tasks you're really good at, that are valuable to the business, but you don't necessarily love doing. An example of this for myself is spreadsheets and financial models. As a trained accountant, I am capable of doing them to a high level of excellence—but I don't love doing them. Excellence tasks can be stopped; however, in my experience you will generally need to invest a little more money into a person or system to achieve this.

The goal is to spend 30 to 40 per cent of your time doing excellence tasks. This leaves 60 to 70 per cent of your time for the Genius Zone.

Genius

The simplest way to describe your Genius Zone is tasks or activities you love to do and are really good at, and if your day was filled with these tasks or activities you would feel energised and happy. Genius Zone tasks are generally easy for you to do and you tend to do them naturally. Your genius zone tasks also tend to be highly profitable.

You will often hear yourself saying 'If only had more time to XYZ, then we would make significantly more money.' Owners of fast growing companies understand this philosophy and understand that the more time spent in the Genius Zone the faster the company will grow.

One of my genius tasks is one-on-one coaching. I absolutely love coaching, I can (and do, at times) coach all day and my energy at the end of the day is the same if not higher than when I started. When you have a day doing the things you love, your energy never seems to waver—in fact, the more you do it the more energy you seem to create.

Remember, you should end up with no more than three to five genius tasks. You want to focus your time on these and delegate the rest.

EXERCISE
1. List the tasks and/or areas of your business you love to work in.
2. List the tasks you avoid or even hate doing.
3. If you could fill your days with the same three to five key tasks, what would they be and why?

CHAPTER 6
THE STOP DOING LIST

I have developed a simple five-step system that allows you to focus on your Genius Zone:

1. Complete a time log.

2. Calculate your hourly rate.

3. Identify your genius.

4. Filter tasks through the Focus Funnel.

5. Write your Stop Doing List.

Step 1: Complete a time log

A time log (as shown in table 6.1, overleaf) is a simple tool used to help you understand where you are spending your time. I recommend you do this for a minimum of two weeks, twice a year. This will give you clarity and insight into what you need to keep doing and, more importantly,

Table 6.1: time log

Time		Monday	Tuesday	Wednesday	Thursday	Friday	Saturday	Sunday
From	To							
05:00	05:15							
05:15	05:30							
05:30	05:45							
05:45	06:00							
06:00	06:15							
06:15	06:30							
06:30	06:45							
06:45	07:00							
07:00	07:15							
07:15	07:30							
07:30	07:45							
07:45	08:00							
08:00	08:15							
08:15	08:30							
08:30	08:45							
08:45	09:00							
09:00	09:15							
09:15	09:30							

what you need to stop doing. You can use the time log tool in the Ultimate Stop Doing List Tool by simply going to www.stopdoing.com.au.

Step 2: Calculate your hourly rate

In order to determine your genius we need to start with a clear measure against which we will evaluate each task. The simplest measure is to understand the dollar value of an hour of your time. When you understand the value of an hour it becomes easier to determine which tasks are worth your time and which ones you need to stop doing.

Work out your hourly rate with this simple mathematical calculation:

1. What is your income goal for the next 12 months? Include your wage and profit from the business.

    _____

2. How many weeks do you intend on working this year? 52 weeks less the number of weeks of holidays you want to take.

    _____

3. How many hours do you intend on working per week? This could be 40, 50 or 60 hours. Be realistic! If you're currently working 80 hours a week it's highly unlikely you'll go to 10 hours a week within the next 12 months.

    _____

The formula is:

$$\text{income} \div \text{weeks} \div \text{hours} = \text{hourly rate}$$

You can use the hourly rate calculator in the Ultimate Stop Doing List Tool by simply going to www.stopdoing .com.au

EXAMPLE:

Mary wants to work out her hourly rate. Over the next 12 months she wants to:

- earn $500 000

- take four weeks of holidays

- only work a 50-hour week.

She would take the $500 000, divide by 48 weeks (i.e. 52 − 4 = 48), and divide that by 50 hours. She would end up with a calculated hourly rate of $208.33 per hour.

Now Mary can use her hourly rate to determine whether she is getting a positive return on investment. If she can get a task done for $20 an hour that she was doing before, she is actually getting a return of $188.33 an hour.

Step 3: Identify your genius

So now that we have a clear measure against which we can evaluate the tasks you are performing, we can identify your genius. The first step is to figure out where you are choosing to spend your time.

Activity inventory

Beyond the time log, the activity inventory is a simple tool that assists you to understand all of the activities you do. The key difference between the time log and the activity inventory is that the latter highlights all the tasks you're doing.

Don't just list the easy-to-remember tasks. Dig deeper to unearth *all* the tasks you do. You might not list answering the phone because it's second nature, yet it's a task that can be delegated (for example, you might employ an assistant or receptionist to be the frontline person to answer the phones — including your mobile phone).

You can use the activity inventory tool in our Ultimate Stop Doing List Tool by simply going to www.stopdoing .com.au

Here are some questions you can ask yourself when you're working on your activity inventory. This is by no means an exhaustive list, but more of a guide to prompt your thinking.

- What aspects of customer service am I personally handling? This can include:
  - answering the phone
  - answering emails
  - entering bookings into the calendar
  - adding contact details to the CRM
  - responding to all customer queries.
- What aspects of sales and marketing am I personally handling? This can include:
  - sales calls
  - networking meetings
  - account management
  - quoting
  - sales presentations

- social media
- copywriting
- updating your website.

• What aspects of administration am I personally handling? This can include:

- entering invoices
- chasing accounts receivable
- processing accounts payable
- handling payroll
- processing payment and petty cash receipts
- handling bookkeeping, such as reconciliation
- handling tax, such as GST
- booking travel.

• What product- and service-related tasks am I handling? This can include:

- working to create your particular product or service
- customer service throughout a project
- quality control.

• What business development tasks am I handling? This can include:

- business planning
- capital expenditure research
- systems development.

- What other general tasks am I personally handling? This can include:
  - cleaning and tidying around the office
  - managing human resources
  - covering work health and safety
  - handling information technology in the office.
- What other tasks do you do? Keep asking until you genuinely can't come up with any more.

Once you have created an extensive list of tasks you perform, you then need to identify the frequency of the task: daily, weekly, monthly or quarterly. If a task is annual, or one-off, simply categorise it as 'other'.

Categorise the activities

Now add a description to each task. Every task should fall into one of the following five categories:

1. Great Financial Return: I am really good at this task, I love doing it and want to KEEP doing it. (These fall in your genius zone.)

2. Great Financial Return: I am really good at this task; I don't love doing it but need to KEEP doing it.

3. Great Financial Return: I am really good at this task; I don't love doing it and want to STOP doing it.

4. Low Financial Return: The task drains me of energy and I resist doing it.

5. Unsure of Financial Return: I know I need to do this task but don't know how.

You can sort them using a table, as shown in table 6.2.

Table 6.2: categorising the activities

Task	Frequency	How long does this task take? (mins)	Description
Emails	Daily	15	*Great Financial Return: I am really good at this task, I love doing it and want to KEEP doing it.*
Calendar booking	Daily	30	*Low Financial Return: The task drains me of energy and I resist doing it.*

The key to describing your tasks is to be able to clearly identify what a great financial return is, together with getting really clear with what you love to do. In my opinion a great financial return means you are performing tasks that directly or indirectly return to you and the business 75 per cent or more of your calculated hourly rate. Tasks that can be performed by someone else for 75 per cent or less than your hourly rate should be done by somebody else so you can maximise your hourly return.

Warning: You can't love every task. Likewise, not every task has a great financial return. You really need to carefully consider the tasks that you record and be your own best critic. Be really hard on yourself and practise applying the 80/20 principle as you work through this part.

From here you will be able to clearly categorise each task into one of the four zones described earlier: Genius,

Excellence, Competence or Incompetence. This is illustrated in table 6.3.

Table 6.3: zoning your tasks

Description	Zone category
Great Financial Return: I am really good at this task, I love doing it and want to KEEP doing it.	Genius
Great Financial Return: I am really good at this task; I don't love doing it but need to KEEP doing it.	Excellence
Great Financial Return: I am really good at this task; I don't love doing it and want to STOP doing it.	Excellence
Low Financial Return: The task drains me of energy and I resist doing it.	Competence
Unsure of Financial Return: I know I need to do this task but don't know how.	Incompetence

Genius categories

You'll usually find genius tasks will fall into one of the following five categories.

1. *Sales.* No matter how good or bad at sales you are, the business owner is almost always the key salesperson in the business. Even if you have a full sales team, there will always be sales that the business owners needs to take the lead on. This might be large corporate accounts, potential buyers, investors or partners, or, even more importantly, selling the business vision and culture to the team. At the end of the day, no-one's going to be quite as passionate about your business as you are.

2. *Marketing*. No business can grow without some form of marketing. Don't make the mistake of thinking marketing is just advertising. Marketing is about:

   - market knowledge
   - identifying target markets
   - product development
   - business culture
   - pricing
   - product delivery
   - product image.

   Even if you're growing your business mainly through referrals, your marketing is how you present your business to people. It's how you create raving fans who want to tell other people about your business.

3. *Team management*. As you build a team, you'll quickly realise how valuable a resource you have in the people who work for you. As with anything of value, you'll need to spend time developing them, training them in their tasks and roles, and generally ensuring they feel valued and important to the business.

4. *Product or service delivery*. I'm not talking about throwing the final product in the back of your car and delivering it. I'm talking about involving yourself in producing the product or service for the client. Most tradespeople will often do this every day. It's often something I debate with many of my coaching clients, since for most business owners this

is the area for which they have the most passion. However, any business where the owner is the primary producer will find itself with a growth ceiling, as the business will struggle to grow beyond the capacity of the owner. For a growing business, at some stage the business owner will need to give up some, if not all, product delivery work, in exchange for continued growth. Often the greatest growth can be seen when the business owner steps aside, allowing talented team members to take on the product delivery, while the owner ensures jobs are delivered to their standard by developing systems.

5. *System development.* For any business owner who wants to have more than merely a job, system development is a must. Here, I'm talking about developing systems to automate tasks and procedures in the business. Building systems helps fuel growth as team members can take on tasks and get the same results each time. Ultimately, it adds value to the business; a well-systemised business is not reliant on the owner, and will be of far greater value to a buyer than one that is completely owner-dependent.

It's unlikely any given business owner will have genius tasks in all areas. However, it's important you either take ownership of these areas personally, or at least put in dedicated staff members to develop each area when it isn't your genius.

Once you have your three to five genius tasks identified, you can move on with the system to create a Stop Doing List, and start delegating to free up time for your genius tasks.

Step 4: Run tasks through the Focus Funnel

In my studies of time management, I came across a book called *Procrastinate on Purpose* by Rory Vaden. In the book, Vaden introduces the concept of the Focus Funnel, which is a mechanism that helps you understand how to multiply your time as opposed to manage your time. The Focus Funnel is made up of several different layers ranging from the tasks you can eliminate, to the ones you can automate and delegate, and finally to the ones that you will procrastinate and the ones you need to concentrate on.

The next step in creating your Stop Doing List is to ask yourself:

1. Can you eliminate this task?
2. Can you automate this task?
3. Can you delegate this task?

If the answer to all these questions is no and it falls through those three filters, it then comes back to you and you have to ask the question: Am I going to concentrate on this now or am I going to procrastinate on it and leave it till later?

Elimination

If you think about a sculptor with a block of stone, when they're trying to chisel out a masterpiece, it's all about elimination. Cut a little bit out here, a little bit out there. We have to take the same mindset with our time. Nothing is as useless as doing efficiently what shouldn't be done at all.

Here are some examples of tasks or things that can be eliminated:

- repeat decisions
- unnecessary meetings
- long emails
- being overly thorough when the bare minimum is all that's required
- Facebook, Twitter or LinkedIn
- very low value tasks.

While that all seems very logical, what is it that stops us from eliminating these things? The emotional side of this is a fear of saying no. We don't want to say no to that meeting, or to crafting a long email. When a task is coming through the filter don't allow the fear to overcome you.

Automation

If it goes through the filter and you can't eliminate it, the next filter is, 'Can I automate this?'

Automation enables you to do something once and have it done repeatedly. It has a compounding effect over time. When we automate, we multiply our time over and over again.

The key to automation is having strong processes, and understanding that if you invest a little bit of extra time today, it's going to save you a lot of time tomorrow. Put simply, in order to automate you need to have great systems and invest in technology that can ensure that the task can operate on autopilot (which is discussed in detail in chapter 9). Again, this sounds very logical, but what's the emotional side of this? Why wouldn't we automate?

One of the big things that often comes up is a fear of technology: I don't understand technology, so I'll just keep doing it the same way because it'll probably be quicker. In order to automate you either need to educate yourself or hire (on a permanent or contract basis) someone who has the skills and knowledge to assist you to automate.

While I know a lot about technology and what it can do for me, I'm not the greatest at implementing technology (some might even call me a technology dinosaur). My role is not to be the technology wiz; my role is to understand how technology can assist the business and instruct others to implement it. It's understanding that there are people around who, for a very affordable price, can help with automation.

The second part of this is a concern with the cost of the automation. The reality is that it's affordable and achievable for everybody in this day and age. You can go on to platforms such as Upwork and find local or overseas talent that will work on a project basis, and will help you set up your automation at a very reasonable rate. You have to apply the mindset that it's going to save you so much time and money in the future by investing a little bit of time and maybe money upfront.

Some things that can be automated might be social media engagement, or having your spam filter set up correctly to eliminate a lot of the clutter coming into your inbox. It might be a 10-second saving here, a minute there, and if you add it all up you'd be saving hours and hours of time a year. Once you multiply that by your hourly rate, you're literally saving thousands of dollars each year.

You could look at other things that can be automated, such as:

- aspects of your sales process
- responses to email queries
- customer service support
- invoicing
- debtor follow-up.

There are so many uses of technology; your entire sales process these days can be automated through CRMs such as Infusionsoft, or by just linking one system to another to ensure data is carried across without human intervention. It doesn't have to be a whole system either; it could be one aspect of an existing system.

Delegation

If you can't eliminate the task, and you can't automate it, then it comes down to the next level: can you delegate it? The only way to delegate is to have people to delegate to. But not just anybody; you want to make sure you have the right people doing the right tasks. If you have the right people, you then need confidence in them and in your systems and training so they can succeed.

Delegation doesn't mean 'every time this task comes in we delegate it'. The *responsibility* has to come off your list, and go onto theirs—and you never see it again. You just know it gets done.

The fears that prevent people from delegating come down to the mindsets discussed in chapter 2:

- I can do it faster myself.

- They won't do it as well as I can.

- It takes too long to train them.

- I've tried this before and failed.

Delegation only fails because of our inability to teach people how to do the task. To successfully delegate you need to learn how to:

- hire the right people (covered in chapter 11)

- give clear instructions and create easy-to-follow systems (covered in chapter 9)

- transmit the correct mindsets (covered in chapters 3 and 11).

Concentrate or procrastinate

If it goes through the filter and you can't eliminate, automate or delegate it, now it's come back to you.

You have to make the decision: Is this something I'm going to focus on and concentrate on now, or can I delay it till later? Be very conscious and deliberate with your decisions, and understand your time is precious. What is the best use of your time right now?

Focus Funnel outcomes

The Stop Doing List system is designed to minimise the number of tasks that get through the filter and require your concentration. Ultimately the only tasks that will be dropping through to you are your genius tasks.

If your Focus Funnel outcome for a task is to eliminate, that's easy enough. If the outcome is to automate, it will require you to combine systems and technology to automate it. And if the outcome is to delegate then you will need a combination of systems and training to delegate it. This is all discussed in detail in chapter 8. You are now ready for the fifth and final stage — creating your Stop Doing List.

Step 5: Write your Stop Doing List

So now you are clear on:

- the value of your time
- where you are choosing to spend your time
- what your genius tasks are
- what you need to eliminate, automate or delegate.

We now have to determine which tasks you are going to stop doing and whether you are ready to stop doing them.

Remember that everything that falls into the Competence and Incompetence zones is considered a task that you *must* stop doing.

Please note that your Stop Doing List is a living document. It is not a one-off exercise. You need to be acutely aware of where you are choosing to spend your time and continuously update your Stop Doing List with tasks you find yourself doing that don't fit into the Genius and Excellence zones.

Also, as you stop doing a task or activity you can remove it from your Stop Doing List as it has now been taken care of.

Table 6.4 is an illustration of the following seven steps. When you take the time to work through each step it will become obvious what you need to stop doing and whether you are ready to stop doing this now.

So let's work through the details of the Stop Doing List system. Take all the tasks that fell into the 'delegate' level of the Focus Funnel.

1. Using your time log, review each task and determine how much time (in minutes) is required to complete the task.

Table 6.4: your Stop Doing List

Task	Frequency	Description	Zone	Focus Funnel Outcome	How long does this task take (mins)	Special Skills Required
Emails	Daily	Great Financial Return: I am really good at this task, I love doing it and want to KEEP doing it.	Competence	Eliminate	15	No
Calendar booking	Daily	Low Financial Return: The task drains me of energy and I resist doing it.	Competence	Delegate	30	Yes

2. Determine whether any special skills are required to complete the task. Examples of specialised skills include industry-specific training, specific software knowledge or requiring certain qualifications or licences to complete the task. This will help you identify whether you have someone on your existing team who can take the task on, or whether you need to employ someone with the required skills.

Task Importance (Low/Med/High)	Is there a system for this task?	Hourly Rate Investment for someone else to do this task	My hourly rate	Net gain/loss	Opportunity cost if you continue to do this task (per annum)	Suggested decision	Are you ready to Stop Doing
Med	No	$ 55.00	208.33	$ 153.33	$ 3680.00	STOP DOING	Not ready
Low	Yes	$ 10.00	$ 208.33	$198.33	$ 9520.00	STOP DOING	Ready to Stop Doing

3. Determine how important the task is to the business. A task is considered of low importance if it wouldn't affect business outcomes were it to be done poorly. High-importance tasks are business critical. Tasks of low importance are easier to stop doing and often require minimal systems and training. It is often at this point that you realise how many of the tasks you choose to do have very little importance to the growth of your business yet seem to take up so much of your time.

4. Calculate the estimated hourly rate investment for someone else to do the task. Put simply, what will you have to pay someone else to do it? You may know this amount. If not, simply estimate how much you will have pay someone per hour to perform the task.

5. Calculate the opportunity cost if you keep doing the task. This is a calculation of how much potential dollar productivity you are giving up by not performing the task. It's a simple calculation:

   Time to perform task (hours) × (your hourly rate - hourly rate of someone else doing the task) × weeks you intend working per year × 2

We multiply it by 2 because there are two costs to the business of you performing the task:

- the cost of your time to perform the task

- the lost income your time could have returned if you invested it in genius tasks.

This is an important point to note because many business owners only consider the cost of their time and justify to themselves that it is cheaper or a better return if they continue to perform the task.

6. If the hourly rate for someone else to perform the task is less than 75 per cent of your calculated hourly rate, you should consider someone else performing it, as you will make more profit from investing your time into your genius.

7. Is there a system for the task? If yes, then you are ready to stop doing it. If not, you are not ready to stop doing it. Pretty simple.

It is important you take the time to download the Ultimate Stop Doing List Tool from www .stopdoing.com.au The tool has been built to assess whether you should stop doing the task, as well as assessing your readiness to stop doing it.

Stop doing the small stuff

It's hard to just stop doing a lot of the tasks in your business. First of all, you need to understand it's a process. I'm not asking you to draw a line in the sand and stop doing everything that's on your Stop Doing List tomorrow. It's going to take time; time to create processes and systems, choose the right people and train them properly.

Secondly, understand the importance of changing your mindset to believe that focusing on these few genius tasks will get you a greater return. You need to develop the internal belief and confidence that less is more, which is the opposite of what you might be used to.

It's been proven, time and time again, in countless industries, whether it's a small, medium or large business, that when we focus and do a few things exceptionally well it creates momentum and success. When we are part of a team that focuses on their tasks or roles, and does their part exceptionally well, the machine will run optimally.

Focusing on your genius takes planning. If you plan out your days, weeks, months and quarters to focus on your genius, then it will happen. Keep in mind, there is no perfect plan. You could plan the perfect day, and have something put you off your game for the rest of the day.

Measure how much time you're spending in your genius before you start to shift into it. Your time log will help here, as it will give you an accurate picture of how you spend your time right now. If you continue to keep your time log, you'll be able to track time spent in your genius and how it improves as you implement the system.

Finally, as challenges or problems arise and you're called upon to resolve them, you need to trust the people you've assigned to solve them. You'll become the coach or director of the people doing the solving. Doing so will teach them how to solve day-to-day problems so they aren't dependent upon you as much anymore.

These are the keys to the Stop Doing List system.

A business owner's projects

Now that you know your genius, how do you choose what projects you spend your time on? This will come back to your goals and what you're trying to achieve. Look at your goals in the long term (three to 10 years), the medium term (the next 12 months) and the short term (the next quarter). This is where your goal setting and planning becomes so important: it gives you a map to where you want to go. You must always consider what needs to happen to move closer to achieving your targets.

A business owner's role will vary from project to project, depending on their genius. My own genius is coaching, presenting or educating, and creating content. So when it comes to presenting, I come up with the content and plan the flow, but I will delegate the preparation of my PowerPoint presentations and the creation and formatting of the handouts. To determine your own role in a project, understand which tasks either fall within your genius or are critically important for you to be part of, and work out how to delegate or outsource the rest.

For some projects you may assign a leader or project manager to oversee the work and be responsible for delivery. You, as the business owner, may be responsible for certain aspects of that project—and inevitably, the buck stops with you—but if you can delegate roles and even leadership of the project, it can help build the team, and take all but your genius tasks off your agenda.

A couple of years ago, we redesigned three of our websites. My assistant was responsible for the delivery and project management of those sites. We sat down and put the project plan together, then assigned tasks to various people with delivery dates.

My assistant was responsible for ensuring each person (including me) had completed their task on time. I had to create some content and sign off on the artwork that was part of the website. My assistant was responsible for the timely delivery of the project, coordinating the web developers, designers and content contributors. It's a great example of how a business owner can work within their genius while also giving employees more ownership (reinforcing their confidence and skills).

Be careful you don't bite off more than you can chew, even when working in your Genius Zone. I've worked with many business owners who look at all the additional time they've created by implementing their Stop Doing List and start taking on a dozen projects. They've just replaced a whole pile of low-value tasks with a large number of high-value tasks, only to find they don't have the time and focus to complete them well.

How many projects a business owner takes on will depend on the phase of business they're in. For example, if you're in start-up phase, you're going to have many moving parts. You've got a lot of new things that you're putting together and you may find you have eight to 12 projects, such as setting up your accounts, launching your marketing campaign, fitting out premises or choosing a logo.

As a general rule I teach that a business should have no more than five projects per quarter and, as an individual, you should not be involved in more than three. Due to the day-to-day operations or challenges you need to handle in growing your business, you can't take on too many projects or you'll struggle to complete those projects well. This is a good guideline that's been tested across companies all over the world, and seems to be a good indicator on workload for a quarter.

Eventually, your genius will become the foundation of each day.

PART III
HOW TO
STOP
DOING

The goal of part III is to get the items you have listed on your Stop Doing List onto somebody else's to-do list.

So; you are now clear on the negative mindsets you need to avoid and the essential mindsets for success. You are clear on what your time is worth and that you need to focus on your Genius Zone to accelerate your growth. You also now have a definitive list of what you need to stop doing and your level of readiness to stop doing.

But how do you actually stop doing?

This next section is designed to help you understand how to take tasks from your Stop Doing List and either eliminate, automate or delegate them so they never end up on your to-do list ever again. Then we'll get into the knowledge–responsibility–control (KRC) model and how you can ensure your delegation is effective.

CHAPTER 7

THE KRC MODEL AND THE STOP DOING LIST

So you've made your Stop Doing List. The knowledge–responsibility–control (KRC) model (as shown in figure 7.1, overleaf) is important to understand in order for the tasks you need to delegate to get completed effectively.

Figure 7.1: the KRC model

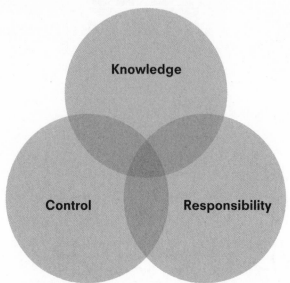

Without knowledge, it is difficult for your staff member to be responsible for something or to control it. Likewise, there is no point for your staff member to try and control something, or know anything about it, without them also having a degree of responsibility for it. And lastly, if they do not have control, it is hard for them to commit to fully knowing or being responsible.

The key to the KRC model is to commit to increasing your staff members':

- knowledge
- responsibility
- control

consistently and systematically, and in the right areas, enabling them to take over the tasks you wish to stop doing.

Knowledge is important

Knowledge is vital to perform any task or function. Without it, things will never get better. You need to know how to do the job. There are ways to do it right and ways to do it wrong. If you don't know the right way to perform a task or activity you will not succeed. You can never know too much, so study, learn, observe, practise.

If you are a business owner or manager, as well as knowing and understanding how to manage, you also need to know what your team is doing. We're not talking about control-freak micromanagement here, just knowing what's going on. I have seen many owners and managers give a task to a team member and pay no further attention, only to have the delivery date arrive with the project in a total shambles. The team member didn't really know what they were doing (lack of knowledge), and the boss didn't catch it because they had no idea what the team member was doing (lack of knowledge). The work and effort is wasted, and the project has fallen behind schedule.

Taking responsibility

When things go wrong you could just say, 'Well, my team member is useless and it's all their fault', or come up with countless other ways to blame others. But we're not talking about blame here. In some companies either the manager or the team member (or both) would be fired for gross incompetence, but that doesn't really benefit anyone. In other companies (particularly those operating a 'no-blame culture' that ends up functioning as 'no-accountability'), the issue would just be swept under the carpet.

Instead, you should look at what went wrong, get some knowledge of the situation, then take some responsibility for it. That opens the door to controlling the situation better through improved training and supervision.

The team member should also take a look and realise that they lack knowledge of the job and of what the manager was looking for. Then they can take some responsibility for the situation and decide to confirm with their manager to ensure they're on the right track next time.

Responsibility means recognising that you have a part to play in making sure things go right, and doing what is needed to make sure they do, rather than finding reasons that explain why they didn't. And if they didn't, it means acknowledging the part you played, so the same thing doesn't happen again (and again and again).

Taking control

Control often gets a bad name when done badly, and has become a bit of dirty word in today's climate. But the fact remains that we all have areas that we need to control, and we must all be willing to be controlled by others in certain areas. A workman must be able to control the tools and machines he uses on the job. At the same time he must be willing to be controlled by his manager, who needs to be able to control such things as what time the workman starts work, what job he is working on today, and so on.

Likewise the manager must be able to exert some control over the workman and at the same time be subject to the control of his senior manager. We are all subject to various controls in the form of regulations and laws, be they the rules of the road, health and safety legislation, or company policies.

An enterprise that is not properly controlled will never get started, veer wildly off course or become a never-ending problem. This applies whether it's a car, a machine, a project or an entire company.

Essentially, control boils down to starting something that needs to get going; changing its speed, direction and so on; keeping it on track; and stopping it when it needs to be stopped. That's exactly what you do when you drive your car, and it's exactly what's needed in managing other people or performing tasks.

Your staff needs to feel control over their tasks. If you are micromanaging and making all the decisions, they won't feel any control, and therefore they won't feel responsible.

Combining the three areas

Knowledge, responsibility, control. All three of these things are needed. Whenever something goes wrong you will find that one of these three things was poor or absent. Understanding which was deficient gives you a head start in remedying the situation. Imagine being given a job, told you are in charge and are responsible for this activity, and yet you don't know the first thing about it. Imagine a project manager being tasked with ensuring a project comes in on time and on budget, yet she is not given control of the resources she needs to work on the project. The personnel she needs all work in other departments for other managers, and she only gets them if they can be spared. Sounds pretty frustrating, right?

Understanding and implementing the KRC model can go a long way to making sure things go right in the first place. But the real value, in my opinion, is that it gives you a roadmap when things haven't gone right. No matter how bad things seem, take some responsibility and put this to work and you will end up in a better, stronger position because you now have more knowledge and will be in better control than ever before.

Applying the KRC model to the Stop Doing List System

How do you get tasks off your Stop Doing List and onto someone else's to-do list? Impart your knowledge and create systems so somebody else can take responsibility of, and control over, the tasks so they ensure that they get done. Figure 7.2 illustrates this.

Figure 7.2: linking KRC

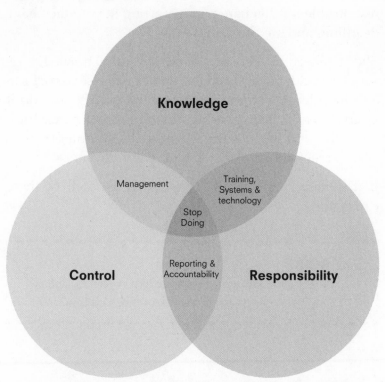

If you look at figure 7.2, the connector between knowledge and responsibility is *training, systems and technology*. In order to impart knowledge and enable someone else to take responsibility, you must have solid systems. Look into how you can use technology and then train the right person and impart your knowledge to them.

The connector between responsibility and control is in having simple *reporting and accountability* in place so you can sleep at night, knowing these tasks are getting done when they are supposed to get done. The people who are responsible for them are now reporting to you; they have deadlines and are accountable.

The connection between control and knowledge is *management*. In order to enable somebody else to perform at a high level, you must manage the process, not do it yourself. Good management structures around meetings, reporting and responsibilities are critically important to ensure these tasks don't stay with you forever.

In the next chapters we look closely at each of these connectors.

EXERCISE
1. Who are the key knowledge holders in your business?
2. Can the business operate without these people?

CHAPTER 8

TRAINING, SYSTEMS AND TECHNOLOGY

Training, systems and technology connect *knowledge* and *responsibility* on the KRC model (see page 93). Combine these three areas to enable automation and delegation, allowing someone else to take responsibility, as shown in figure 8.1, overleaf. Remember, the goal is to help you to spend more time in your Genius and Excellence zones. In order to get to the heart of your Genius Zone, we need to incorporate knowledge, responsibility and control.

Figure 8.1: training, systems and technology

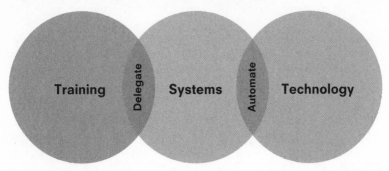

Training

Training your people is essential for the Stop Doing List system to work. So often business owners think that training is all about sending somebody on a course or simply quickly showing them what needs to be done—once. The reality is that training is a continuous process for business owners. If you're not committed to training your people, both initially and on an ongoing basis, you can't expect them to perform tasks at the level you expect.

When moving an item off your Stop Doing List it is essential to be clear on:

- what the outcome of the task is
- the specific result you're looking for
- how the task fits into the big picture of your business.

Document the process in as much detail as possible, so someone with no knowledge about the task can follow the steps and perform the task. The best way to document a process is to actually perform the task yourself, and write down each step you do along the way, like a recipe. You need to identify if the team member needs to have any particular skill sets or information, and whether there's anything else that might be required before they take on the task; and then list the method step by step.

Now that you have a documented system, you will need to identify who is going to be responsible for the task or system and train that person. You will need to allocate sufficient time to do this. As you train, record what you're doing. You can even use your smartphone's voice recorder app and create training videos or audio so the person you're training can go back and listen and watch the training again. This has the added benefit of removing the need to repeat yourself over and over again.

Training requires you to have systems and procedures in place that you can teach others. This training can be in many forms, including:

- written
- audio
- video
- face-to-face.

Training is all about:

- spending time with people
- showing them how to perform the task
- instructing them to follow the system
- showing them the end result.

It requires you to be an excellent communicator and to understand that people learn in different ways and at different speeds.

Some common training mistakes are:

- not spending enough time on training
- assuming that the trainee has understood 100 per cent of the material and can now work independently
- creating boring and non-interactive training materials
- focusing too much on the theory and not enough on the practice
- not providing enough detail to enable the trainee to succeed.

Your training should answer the questions you ask yourself in your head when you perform the task. It should teach your people how to overcome common obstacles that can't be systemised and give them the knowledge to take ownership and responsibility.

The four stages of learning a new skill

It is important to note at this point that there are four definitive stages to learning a new skill, as shown in figure 8.2. These stages come from a classic psychological approach and follow what an individual goes through to master any skill. They are:

1. unconscious incompetence
2. conscious incompetence
3. conscious competence
4. unconscious competence.

Figure 8.2: the four stages of learning

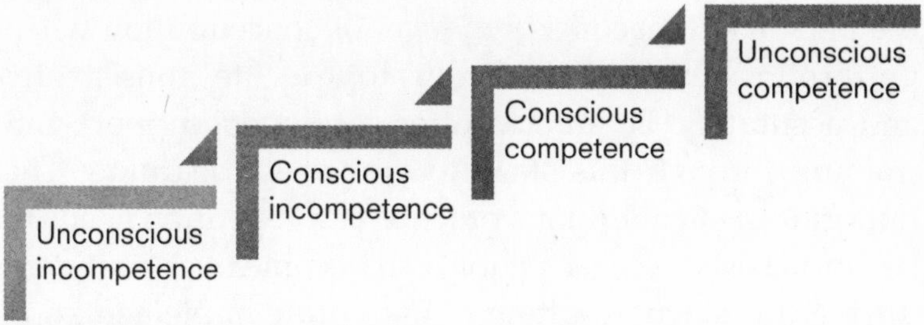

Stage labels: Unconscious incompetence, Conscious incompetence, Conscious competence, Unconscious competence

Stage 1: unconscious incompetence

Put simply, at this stage you or the person you are delegating to does not know how to perform a specific task, and there is no recognition that there is even a knowledge gap regarding the task. In other words, in this stage you don't know what you don't know!

Stage 2: conscious incompetence

In stage 2 you are now aware that you or the person you are training needs to learn new skills. During this stage the person becomes acutely aware of their shortcomings and will either run and hide under a rock or step up to the challenge to learn the new skills. During stage 2, ensure you are choosing the best person to invest your time in training. If they do not have a willingness and openness to learning new skills then it will be a hard road to success (if you get there at all!).

Stage 3: conscious competence

At stage 3 the person being trained has now acquired the new skills and knowledge to perform the tasks assigned. They are putting their learning into practice and are able to perform tasks to an average to high standard. However, the person still needs a high level of concentration when performing the task in order to execute consistently and accurately. Be sure to offer continued support and training through this stage to embed the learning. The importance of continuous practice and repetition needs to be emphasised also, as people can become over-confident during this stage, resulting in inaccurate implementation of the new skill. This is the stage where most learning or training stops and why the tasks inevitably end up back on your to-do list. When you break through stage 3 and move to stage 4 you can be confident you can stop doing the task or activity forever.

Stage 4: unconscious competence

You know you have reached stage 4 when the skill or task you have learnt is now second nature and you can perform the tasks without having to 'think' too much. The tasks can be performed with speed, accuracy and consistency.

This is the level of skill required for tasks and activities to never come back on to your to-do list.

In order to stop doing tasks you need to be committed to training others and supporting them through to stage 4. It's important to note that you generally have stage 4 skill in most of the tasks you want to delegate and outsource, yet you often forget how you got to that stage. It's a process and takes time.

The five keys to successful training

Training takes time and needs to be done in a way that enables people with different learning styles to understand. You need to incorporate different forms of communication as you train—try a combination of video, audio or written formats, for example.

Here are five keys to successfully train your people, regardless of their learning style:

1. *'Hire for attitude, train for skill.'* That's a quote from author and management guru Tom Peters. It is my experience that trying to change the personality or attitude of an individual is challenging, if not impossible in most cases. You need to employ people with the right attitude and personality—the skills can be taught.

2. *Slow down to speed up.* This seems counterintuitive for most business owners, as they are trying to speed up and get more done each day. However, trying to teach too many things at once will inevitably lead to failure and cost you more time and money in the long run. Train your people in one to two skills at a time, allow them to practice to the point that they can complete the task 70 to 80 per cent as well as you can—then move on to the next skill.

3. *Check in on progress.* Most training in organisations is done once, with very little ongoing support and follow-up. Whenever you train a new skill, you need to plan multiple check-in points to assess how well that person is executing the new skill, and provide additional training and support as

necessary. New skills don't become habit overnight. They require practice and refinement. The first 60 to 90 days after the initial training are the most critical. I would plan for weekly check-ins so you can assess and refine the skills. To quote Vince Lombardi, 'practice does not make perfect. Only perfect practice makes perfect.'

4. *Implement a simple scoreboard.* 'What gets measured gets done.' In order to speed up the process of your people learning and integrating a new skill, you must measure the results of the application of that skill. Simple measures such as 'time to complete task' or 'percentage compliance to the system' are easy to implement.

5. *Measure progress.* If you do all of the above, you should be able to observe the person learning the new skills improve as they become more confident and the new skill becomes second nature. If you are not seeing incremental improvement then you need to assess your training (content and method) and the amount of support you are providing to reinforce the new skill.

What to cover

When you are training people to take over a task, it is important you don't just run them through the steps. It is critical that you teach your people how you think when you are implementing the task. Hence, when you train your people you must include the following:

1. *Define success and the benefits.* You need to clearly articulate what success looks like. You can't achieve something you can't visualise.

2. *Define failure and the costs.* Most people are unaware of the direct and indirect costs to the business of not implementing or performing the task well.

3. *The dos and don'ts.* You need to be clear what the person can do without you and what they should come to you about. For example, after completing a step of the task or activity should they wait to be told what to do next, or simply move to the next step and report their progress to you?

4. *The clear recipe for success.* The instructions need to be thorough yet simple and easy to follow. This is ideally in written or video form, and have checklists if possible.

5. *Be prepared!* In almost all cases there will be a list of common obstacles to be aware of. Making your people aware of these, together with training them how to solve the problem, will increase their chance of success.

6. *Clear communication and deadlines.* Be sure to agree on how you will communicate throughout the implementation of the task, together with timelines for task completion. I also suggest scheduling check-in points (I suggest either daily or weekly, depending on the task or project) to review progress and answer any questions.

Once you've trained the employee, get them to repeat back their understanding of the task and what you're asking of them, and get them to step through the task in real time. This gives you the opportunity to be clear on whether they understand and are actually doing it the way you want it to be done. It also enables you to correct anything they may have heard wrong or interpreted differently to how you meant it.

Inspect the results

The last step is a quote I learned very early in business: 'You can only expect what you inspect.' Many business owners make the mistake of taking someone through their training too quickly and sending them on their way, never inspecting the task or output until there's a problem.

I'm not talking about micromanagement, but rather checking that they're implementing the system the way you trained them to. You need to debrief them after the first few times they've done the task so you can be sure they're doing it the way you've taught them (or perhaps they're doing it better, and you need to improve your training).

As a general rule of thumb, if someone can do a task I've taught them three times without any input, I feel comfortable and confident they can then own that task and be responsible for it.

I will still do periodic inspection, maybe every one to three months, to ensure it's still being done correctly, because accountability is still important.

Systems

Systemising your business is one of the most important yet undervalued elements in protecting your business' short- and long-term success. This may come as a surprise to you, but it is an area that, despite its simplicity, most business owners avoid like the plague.

Now you may have heard that without systems you don't *own* a business—you *are* the business. But why does this matter? Well, if you don't have systems and your goal is to double your revenue, then logic would tell us that you need to double the hours you work. Now most of the business owners I meet for the first time are already working 60, 70 or even 80-plus hours per week. So working more hours is unrealistic and will limit how fast and how big your business can grow.

Fortunately, if you are automating where possible, delegating as much as feasible and systemising the majority of your business processes, you can create a high-growth business.

A systems mindset is essential irrespective of whether your business is in the startup phase or is well established. From my experience, business systems are neglected by business owners because:

- they are certainly not seen as sexy or exciting (in fact some may go as far as saying that good business systems are boring)

- business owners believe there is no urgency to create them until something is going wrong or they are ready to stop doing a task.

While business owners seem to have a never-ending to-do list, and all of these important tasks are vying for the limited time of one person (YOU), please believe me when I say the longer you neglect systemising your business the harder it will be for you to stop doing anything.

Systemisation starts with unpacking your brain and documenting how you do what you do. These processes, policies, and procedures may then be collected and distributed as a manual to show how you do what you do in the business. I recommend that you don't limit this to documenting only *what* you do but also documenting *how* all tasks and activities are carried out. You want to document the why, what, when, where, who and how of each task, process and activity required to operate your business.

If a task is going to be done more than once in a business it requires a system. The benefits of building a business that is systemised include:

- increased productivity as your team understand how to carry out tasks correctly without needing to bother you with questions

- enhanced customer experience as systems ensure consistent delivery that inevitably results in higher average spend per customer and increased repeat business

- increased staff accountability through clear and simple measurement of their performance

- decreased dependence on the business owner.

Systems are a *must* when it comes to the Stop Doing List; without them you will fail. The most valuable business systems are those that are replicable. If your business is built on the back of your talent, then you can't scale it.

There are four key areas to focus on when you start building your business systems: marketing, sales, operations and administration. This is applicable to all businesses, irrespective of the sector they operate in:

- *Marketing.* The systems that support your business in generating a consistent flow of leads and enquiries.

- *Sales.* A set of strategic and very deliberate steps that assist lead nurturing, follow-up and conversion.

- *Operations.* The systems that result in consistent service or product delivery to your customers. These often include customer service systems.

- *Administration.* This includes accounts, reception, human resources and so on.

Rules for creating systems

Most business owners I meet have little if any idea how to create effective systems for their business. Here is a simple set of rules to apply when creating systems.

1. Is this task repeatable? If yes, then begin.

2. The title should always begin with 'How to'.

3. Always give short, clear and concise written instructions that communicate the steps to take, including screenshots where needed.

4. Whenever possible provide a video walk-through. (It should not take longer than five minutes to explain in a video; if it takes longer than that, consider breaking up the video into two parts.)

5. Include:
   - even the most obvious steps
   - where to find usernames and passwords
   - clickable links to relevant URLs.

6. Before finalising the system, have a staff member review the system and go through the process.

7. Incorporate the feedback, editing, adding or removing any steps.

When writing systems, constantly think: if a person off the street were to read the steps, could they execute the task without asking anyone any questions? If you are struggling with creating a particular system, first check online to see if you can find any resources that can help you. If you can't find anything ask your team for assistance.

You need to share these rules with anyone in your business who will be writing systems. This will ensure consistency and accuracy of the systems being created.

Checklists are key

A great tool to consider when building the systems in your business is checklists. Checklists are generally easy to create and follow. They make recall easy and tend to set out the minimum steps necessary to complete a task.

Making checklists is often viewed as tedious and boring, but I can guarantee they will save you and your business a lot of money by improving efficiency and minimising mistakes. Also, with checklists there's a trail (paper or electronic) showing accountability for each step of a task. If checklists are used in your business, you will find tasks will be completed more consistently and challenges will be pinpointed before they become big and often expensive problems.

In the book *The Checklist Manifesto* by Atul Gawande, Daniel Boorman of the Boeing Company in Seattle says of checklists:

> Good checklists are precise. They are efficient, to the point, and easy to use even in the most difficult situations. They do no try to spell out everything—a checklist cannot

fly a plane. Instead, they provide reminders of only the most critical and important steps—the ones that even the highly skilled professionals using them could miss. Good checklists are, above all, practical.

This quote provided a moment of inspiration for me in relation to the Stop Doing List System. Checklists are a great complement to your detailed systems. A good checklist will capture the steps that are critical to successfully implementing the system and yet they seem so simple that they are often easy to forget or overlook.

Technology

No matter the size of your business or the stage of the business life cycle you are at, technology is critical to your business success. It is also essential to the Stop Doing List system, as it can aid in the automation of many tasks.

Technology can be quite daunting for many business owners. There are so many different functions that technology can assist with and so many choices in each area; it's so overwhelming that it seems easier to continue to do things the same old way. But continuing with business as usual means your business can't grow.

Choosing the best technology to adopt can be challenging. It is often so difficult to match the best technological solutions to a business's particular set of problems that many business owners avoid making a decision simply to avoid making the *wrong* decision.

To avoid feeling overwhelmed by technology and paralysed in your decision making, you need to be strategic in your technology choices. Only invest in new technology if it aligns with a clearly defined process you want to automate and you are clear on how the new technology will help. Lastly, remember that technology can't compensate for poor or nonexistent systems.

Technologies that help you stop doing

When working with your team, especially in a virtual environment, picking the right technology for the task can be quite tricky, considering the wide range of options available. Often the choice will come down to personal preference, or even just the small benefits one technology will have over a competitor.

Most technologies will have some kind of trial period, during which you can evaluate them to ensure they're the right fit. Sometimes you need to dive in and try it out to see if the time and money savings it brings to your business are worth the investment.

Important considerations about tools are:

- *Ease of use.* The technology needs to be easy for your team members to use, or they won't use it. As with any system, if it makes life easier, they will use it, but if it doesn't, they will generally avoid it.

- *Range of benefits.* Each tool needs to cover your specific area. Even the best tool for a particular task may not fit you well if it doesn't cater to your specific requirements.

- *Ability to integrate.* Ideally you want the technologies you use to talk to one another to avoid double handling of information.

- *Cost*. These tools cost money to develop and deploy. Research your options and use reviews to help determine which is the right choice. There are usually experts who can also help you set up your tools so you can get the most out of them, faster.

Let's go into the technologies from a few different categories. This is by no means an exhaustive list (that would be a book on its own).

Calendar management and scheduling tools

Keeping your calendar organised is a top priority, both for meeting times and for personal blocks of time to get things done. These are the top tools for managing your calendar and scheduling appointments so you can be more productive:

- TimeTrade (www.timetrade.com)
- Calendly (www.calendly.com)
- ScheduleOnce (www.scheduleonce.com)
- Eventbrite
- Google Calendar
- YouCanBook.me

Any business that deals with bookings can benefit from great booking software. They will often have features that allow a team member to set all available time slots for meetings, from which the client can then choose the best time for them.

Project management and communication tools

There are many tools available to help you manage your team members. If we start with your overseas team members, you'll often need a project management tool, something like:

- *Asana*. A team collaboration–based project management tool.

- *Basecamp*. One of the more popular project management tools.

- *Trello*. A minimalist project tool based on the Kanban paradigm. It uses multiple lists with tasks to manage projects.

- *Slack*. A free communication tool, Slack supports real-time messaging, archiving and search.

- *Dropvox*. Note the v — this is one of my favourite tools. It's an iPhone app that allows you to record audio clips and load them automatically into your Dropbox. It is great for dictating letters, notes, emails or even blog posts.

- *Voxer*. This works a bit like a walkie-talkie, however it also has integrated text, photo and location sharing that can be sent alongside voice messaging. Great for quick messages while you're on the run.

- *Viber*. This app allows you to make free calls and send text and picture messages to other Viber users for free (all you need is an internet connection).

These are really communication methods, enabling the team to see what tasks are due, when they're due, and manage the project based on those tasks. The beauty of these and many other project management tools is they're free for smaller teams, they have nice apps that go with them and they enable you to communicate in real time with your teams and see what's going on.

File sharing, email and document collaboration tools

It's hard to work with any virtual team without an easy and controllable way to share and collaborate on files. These include:

- *Dropbox*. An excellent file-sharing app.

- *Microsoft Office and OneDrive*. One of the most popular office software suites. It's quite familiar to many users and there's plenty of training available. Email handling is available through the Office 365 subscription.

- *Gmail, Google Docs and Drive*. A Microsoft alternative that allows excellent live collaboration on documents. It's an excellent email system with very strong anti-spam measures available.

- *DocuSign*. With DocuSign, documents can be shared and electronically signed.

Training tools

Whenever you're creating training aids and systems, you need good recording tools to help communicate what you're teaching. An example is Camtasia, great screen-recording software that helps you to create video tutorials along with recorded audio. I also use Camtasia if I need to explain specific projects or tasks to my team that are quite complex. This really helps with their understanding and often reduces the number of questions I get asked around how to execute a project or task.

Meeting tools

Communication is key when working with a virtual team, and having inexpensive, reliable software through which to conduct your meetings is important. Examples include:

- *Skype.* You can use Skype for both video conferencing and phone conversations, as well as instant messaging. It's a really good way to communicate with your overseas and local people. You can even set up your virtual team members with an Australian phone number to make and receive cheap calls on, wherever they are in the world.

- *Google Hangouts.* This is free software for video conferencing and group meetings with up to 10 participants.

- *GoToMeeting or Zoom.* These are generally used for longer meetings that will involve multiple people; they are more stable at times than Skype, however they are also more expensive. You can easily record meetings for future reference.

Customer relationship management

Customer relationship management (CRM) systems may not usually be considered a key teamwork tool. However, they're important tools for allowing the team to collaborate when working with clients. They provide a central place team members can record information about clients, accessible to other team members if needed. It's quite important to ensure the business isn't relying on

one person with specialised knowledge about a client.
Examples of CRMs are:

- *Infusionsoft*. This is one of the leading marketing
  automation tools for small to medium businesses.
  Infusionsoft also has an integrated database
  designed to work with its marketing automation.
  The combination of both tools can help many
  businesses grow and implement sales systems.

- *Salesforce*. Salesforce has one of the most
  sophisticated CRMs on the market, with options to
  cater for small businesses right up to corporate-level
  customer management.

- *Highrise*. This was built to organise emails,
  conversations, notes, proposals, and so on. You
  can receive reminders to follow up on calls, attend
  meetings, or reply to an email.

Email tools

Email is a way of life now. It is important to have email
tools that enable you to run your day-to-day
email correspondence, together with managing your
email broadcasts to your database. Examples of email
tools are:

- *Google apps for business*. This is a great tool that
  enables you to access your email as long as you
  have an internet connection and access to a browser.
  This is extremely useful when you want an assistant
  to start managing your emails for you.

- *Mailchimp*. Great for creating and sending email
  marketing campaigns. Mailchimp can also help you
  collect email addresses and manage your email list.

Marketing technologies

Gone are the days of requiring expert coders and technological wizards. It's never been easier to set up and measure your marketing campaigns. You can have professional-looking marketing on the web within minutes with the right tools. There are literally thousands of tools you can use to assist you in this area—here are three of my favourites:

- *Google Analytics.* This can be used to track a variety of website statistics. It helps you to understand your customers. It may seem like a foreign language at first but once you get a basic understanding it will really help you understand and measure your marketing effectiveness.

- *Leadpages.* This is a simple landing page and email opt-in form generator that integrates with a variety of email service providers. Leadpages gives you access to optimised and mobile-responsive landing page templates and allows you to test which pages lead to more click-throughs.

- *OptimizePress.* This is a simple WordPress plugin that allows you to easily create professional and high-converting landing pages, sales pages and membership portals.

Productivity tools

Understanding which tools to use to save you time is a must in today's day and age. Here are some examples of tools that can increase your productivity:

- *Evernote.* This app uses the cloud to allow you to share and sync notes and files. A quick and easy way to capture any flash of inspiration or idea—it's as simple as creating a notebook and saving the notes in there.

- *StayFocusd.* This is a free browser extension that allows you to block time-killing websites, enabling you to stay on task and ultimately get more done. You can configure it to your personal needs but the basic premise is to 'lock you out' of the distracting sites you choose, denying you the choice to be distracted.

- *IFTTT.* The name stands for 'if this then that'. This software allows you to create 'recipes' to streamline activities and increase productivity. While it may only save you a few minutes here or there, once set up it will save you hours and ultimately thousands of dollars each year. The software integrates with many online platforms including Dropbox, Twitter, Facebook, LinkedIn, Evernote, Gmail, Google Calendar, WordPress, and many more.

- *Zapier.* Much like IFTTT but more business focused, this software helps you connect and automate applications with custom-defined sequences and rules.

- *RescueTime.* Much like a time log, RescueTime helps you understand where you are spending your time online and on your computer. It also allows you to record what you did when you were offline, giving you a great picture of where you choose to invest or waste your time.

***

So as you can see, training, systems and technology are critical to the success of the Stop Doing List system. You need to invest your time into implementing the right combinations of these so you can automate or delegate tasks from your Stop Doing List. However, this section only provides a link between knowledge and responsibility in the KRC model. In the next chapter I will show you how to bridge responsibility and control.

EXERCISE

1. List the tasks you wish to delegate.
   - Do they have a documented system? (Written, video or audio?)
   - Do you have someone on your current team who would be suitable to train for this task?
   - How much time will you allocate per week/month to train someone to learn the new skill?
   - What do you feel is a reasonable time frame to learn the new skill?
2. List the tasks you wish to automate.
   - Do they have a documented system? (Written, video or audio?)
   - Are you aware of technology that exists to help you automate this task?
   - How much time will you allocate per week/month to implement the new technology?
   - What do you feel is a reasonable time frame to implement the new technology?

CHAPTER 9
REPORTING AND ACCOUNTABILITY

Reporting and accountability are essential for you to understand what is going on in your business and ensure tasks are getting done at the correct time and to the standard you expect. Regardless of the size of your business, having your team report to you regularly will be a great measure of their productivity and will inevitably improve yours. Now, don't stress and think that the reporting I'm talking about is going to be more work. In fact, reporting will be a vehicle that will allow you to:

- motivate your team members to make regular, measurable progress

- answer any questions or be clear on where your team needs your assistance

- invite your team to provide suggestions and give feedback on what is working and not working.

Without an effective reporting process in place it is quite challenging to understand if your team is doing a good job and moving in the right direction. This then leads to many unnecessary conversations and emails so you can understand what is going on. This takes a lot of time and can be quite frustrating. You may feel out of control and uneasy instead of feeling in control and clear about what is going on in your business each day.

A good reporting rhythm is essential. I recommend three key reports—daily, weekly and monthly—to provide you with clarity about what each person is doing and responsible for, along with confidence that these tasks are getting done when you need them to be done.

Daily reports

The daily report is designed to give you an understanding of what your team member has achieved during that day. The report answers three questions:

1. What did you accomplish today?

2. Did you achieve everything that was scheduled to be completed today? (If no please list what wasn't completed and why it wasn't completed.)

3. Is there anything you need help with or do you have any questions?

These questions are designed to keep your people focused on the specific tasks that have been assigned to them and also ensure that they are performing their assigned tasks in a timely fashion. It also allows for open dialogue on a daily basis to ensure that tasks and projects are moving forward and aren't delayed because of you.

Weekly reports

The weekly report is designed to be a summary of the week's activities. Each person needs to report on the success or failure of achieving their key responsibilities and report to you their weekly KPIs. This report will also include answers to the following questions:

- What was your brightest moment of the week?
- What was your biggest challenge of the week?
- What did you learn in the last week?
- Based on the week gone by I believe we should STOP DOING…
- Based on the week gone by I believe we should START DOING…
- I need your help with…

This report will form a good part of the agenda for your weekly meeting you have with your team. The report is designed to allow you to gauge how each person is feeling throughout their work week, together with giving you valuable feedback and ideas on how to continue to grow and develop your business.

Monthly reports

The monthly report is designed to be a mini 360-degree assessment of the person's performance. The team member will list each task that has been assigned to them, the frequency of the task and the importance of the task. They will then list the date they were trained in the task and who trained them. The person completing the report will then give themselves a score out of 10 on their ability to complete the task with 100 per cent confidence and trust.

This report will then be submitted to the team member's direct manager (this may be you or somebody else) for them to assess. Once the assessment is complete it is essential that a meeting occur to discuss the assessment score variances and how these will be rectified. This will often involve retraining or further system development.

Accountability

Accountability often gets confused with someone taking the blame for something. This is not what we are talking about here. Accountability is in my opinion about delivering on a commitment. It's being answerable or responsible to someone for something. It is essential to your ability to stop doing the tasks on your list that someone becomes accountable for the task or activity.

In order to achieve this it is essential to implement the following five steps:

1. *Set clear expectations.* Your people can only be accountable to the level to which they understand what is expected of them. Hence it is important to be clear about the outcome you desire, the time frame you require this to be completed, and whether you require them to follow a specific system to achieve the outcome or they can choose their own adventure.

2. *Arm them with the tools of success.* Make sure your people are trained and have all the tools they require to achieve the desired outcome; otherwise you are setting them up to fail.

3. *Create a simple scoreboard of performance.* While you may discuss the specific outcome you desire, it is important to establish some milestone check-ins and progress reports to enable you and the person performing the task or project to clearly understand whether they are 'winning'.

4. *Conduct constructive feedback sessions.* Open, honest and constructive feedback is essential to ensure your people understand how they are performing. This is made easier by implementing steps 1 to 3. This will at times require some tough conversations, but remember the only way for your people to get better is for them to understand what they need to improve.

5. *Establish clear rewards and consequences.* Most
    accountability is ineffective because there are
    no clear rewards or consequences for following
    through on what you said you were going to do.
    If a person has succeeded then they should be
    rewarded in some way. This could be a simple as
    acknowledging their achievement, or if they prove
    themselves over time it may lead to a promotion.
    If they have not followed through and delivered
    on their commitment, and you feel confident you
    have set them up to succeed, then you might need
    to consider assigning the task or activity to someone
    else or perhaps even moving the person on.

While this may seem simple to follow and execute, this
simple five-step process is often neglected. Please take
the time to understand and implement this—you will be
amazed at how quickly you see a positive return.

CHAPTER 10
MANAGEMENT

Management is the link between *control* and the *knowledge* in the KRC model. Being a great manager takes time, patience and persistence. There are many different management styles that work and it is important that you get clear on your own management style. However, regardless of your specific management style, there are some specific characteristics that all great managers possess. Great managers are:

- *Motivated.* They seem to love what they do. In particular they are motivated to build a team and help their team succeed.

- *Motivating.* They exude a positive energy that inspires and motivates their team to work hard.

- *Confident.* They are confident in their decisions and in their people.

- *Knowledgeable.* They tend to commit to continuous and never-ending learning practices, resulting in them being aware of current best practices and trends.

- *Respectful*. They show the same level of respect to all team members irrespective of performance or position title.

- *Trusting*. They understand that in order to get the best from their team they have to trust them to perform in their role.

- *Direct and honest*. They aren't afraid to have the tough conversations with people. Their communication is always clear, constructive and concise.

- *Flexible and adaptable*. They understand that not everything is going to go to plan. They are often prepared for this and lead their team through the challenges to deliver on the agreed outcome.

- *Grateful*. They appreciate the efforts of their team and regularly communicate this to their team. Whether it's small daily wins or the achievement of a larger strategic objective, great managers will be sure to sincerely thank their team.

Another aspect of being a great manager is ensuring you set your team up to win. What do I mean by this? Too often as business owners we are moving fast. We have so many things to do each day that we can be vague when we delegate tasks to others and simply expect that our people will know what to do. Then when they 'fail' we have thoughts like, 'Why did I hire this person when I could easily be doing this work myself and saving the money!' So to set your people up to win, I recommend you develop a management system that includes:

- being clear with the outcome you expect
- providing an example or demonstration of what you want
- setting clear benchmarks and checkpoints along the way that will help both of you understand if the project or task is on track and meeting the expected standard
- allowing people to do their job freely by not micromanaging, which often leads to people being nervous and not performing their best work.

You want to be a fair manager who doesn't have to micromanage, get upset with your team, or use overly direct language to get things done. It is essential for you to become a great communicator and understand that your ability to set your people up will ultimately determine their success or failure.

Meeting rhythm

The key to great management, whether your staff are local or overseas, virtual or in your workplace, is regular communication and a good meeting rhythm. You need to think of these meetings like the pulse of your business. If it's not beating regularly and rhythmically, then inevitably you'll get an unhealthy system.

In the 15 years I've spent working in or with growing companies, the companies who are consistently growing and achieving their goals are those that have established a routine and rhythm of having meetings. The faster they are growing, the more meetings they have. Now while this may sound counterintuitive and even crazy to you, I need to clarify that I'm not talking about having a meeting for the sake of having a meeting. I'm talking about having short meetings that are run to time, with a specific structure and agenda.

Most meetings are poorly run, demotivating and, to be frank, a waste of everyone's time. If run properly, your meetings will be inspiring and positive and enable the business to grow at a faster rate.

A big key to running successful meetings is to prepare for them properly. This is why the daily, weekly and monthly reports are so important. The reports are designed to give you the information required to run a short and productive meeting. This way the meeting can cut through the information-gathering stage that often takes up the majority of most meetings and get straight into constructive discussions and/or sharing.

A great meeting rhythm that I have implemented with many companies is:

- daily meeting (or sometimes referred to as a daily huddle)
- weekly meeting
- monthly meeting.

Daily meeting (huddle) – a must in growing companies

A daily meeting or huddle is a short meeting (five to 15 minutes) designed to support discussions around tactical issues and provide short updates. This is a great way to bring everyone together, keep everyone focused and build a culture of camaraderie and teamwork.

While this may seem like overkill and not necessary, this is a practice that many fast-growing companies around the world have implemented and are practising on a daily basis. You may feel like you don't have the time to conduct such a meeting, or feel you are having enough interactions already so you don't need another meeting. In my experience, when implemented well, the daily huddle will save you time, reduce impromptu conversations and increase the efficiency of information sharing.

I have worked with many organisations that have implemented this well and the results are immediate. Your team will be more aligned, and you will be able to control the internal energy together with accelerating the growth of your company. Let me delve a little deeper on the structure and limits that lead to a successful daily huddle.

Timing

It is recommended that you set the start of the daily huddle at an odd time, such as 10.10 am or 12.12 pm, to make it memorable. Starting at an odd time often leads to people being on time, believe it or not. As this is quite a short meeting you don't really have very much time to waste. So it is important to the success of the huddle that you start and finish on time (ideally the meeting shouldn't go for longer than 15 minutes). In the beginning I recommend getting someone to time the meeting and to end the meeting regardless of whether the agenda is finished or not.

Setting

In order to the keep the meeting short it is best to conduct the daily huddle standing up. This keeps the energy high and will help you to avoid extending the conversation—people don't want to have to stand for too long.

Participants

Verne Harnish, author of *Scaling Up* and one of the leading pioneers of the daily huddle concept, says, 'In general, the goal is to have more people in less meetings, not more meetings with less people.' It is for that reason that I recommend you involve the maximum number of staff members. The ideal number to keep the meeting short and allow a good exchange of information is 10 to 20 people. In larger companies I would recommend you create a daily huddle in each department, and another daily huddle with the heads of the departments.

Agenda

The last point to consider is the heart of the daily huddle; the questions. The agenda should be the same every day, and is only three items long (allowing up to five minutes per item). An agenda that has worked with many of my clients revolves around the following three questions:

1. Did you achieve your primary focus yesterday?
2. What is your primary focus today?
3. What obstacles will keep you from completing it/ Where are you stuck?

The meeting rhythm will depend on the role and on the organisational culture. Depending on what other meetings are scheduled, I usually have a daily meeting with my personal assistant. That daily meeting is critical to her role and her ability to support me in what I'm doing. Those meetings are pre-booked in my diary, one month in advance.

It's a 15-minute meeting, and the conversation starts with 'How can I help?', and my assistant will give all the updates for the day. The meeting shifts when she says 'Matt, how can I help you?' and then I update her on what I need done. While hosting this meeting, we use Asana (our project management tool). We both have it open and make changes in real time, so we can both see the capture of those tasks and make sure they get managed properly.

Weekly and monthly meetings

The second meeting type is the weekly meeting, which is a 50-minute meeting with a clear agenda that talks about the critical progress updates within a business. It engages conversation to help people understand, and gathers feedback from the team on what the business should keep doing, stop doing and start doing.

When it comes to one-on-one, team, weekly or any other meetings that follow an agenda, culturally it's good to start with:

- What are your wins for the week and why do they matter?

- What has been your biggest challenge and why does it matter?

- What have you learnt in the past week and how can you apply it?

This helps set a positive mood and tone for the meeting, providing a chance to celebrate individual victories as a team and praise individuals in front of the team. 'Wins and positives' for the week could be the first item on your meeting agenda. From there, move on to the remaining items.

I always end my weekly meetings with these two questions:

1. As an organisation, based on the past seven days, what should we STOP doing?

2. As an organisation, based on the past seven days, what should we START doing?

These two questions allow people to voice their concerns or frustrations as well as provide ideas or solutions that can enhance the business.

Monthly meetings follow a similar agenda to the weekly meetings, except you need to add a strategic layer to it. By this I mean you should check in with the company's goals and solve any major challenges to enable you to continue moving forward.

CHAPTER 11
THE RIGHT STAFF

The final piece of the Stop Doing List puzzle is to find the right staff to work with you and take over a lot of the tasks that appear on your Stop Doing List. In this chapter we'll discuss the recruitment process itself. Recruitment is far more than holding interviews with as many people as possible until you find the best of the bunch. It's about knowing the:

- parameters of the role

- location for the role, be it local or remote

- personality for the role

- fit for your business culture

- category for the position — is it role-based or task-based?

Once you've found the right fit, later in this chapter we'll look towards onboarding your new team member, to help them feel welcome to your team. Finally, when it comes to recruitment, you may have heard the phrase, 'hire slow, fire fast'. When you take your time with the recruitment process to find the right person, and be ready to let go of the wrong people, you'll have fewer issues in the long run. However, sometimes moving a staff member on is unavoidable; this chapter will cover that as well.

Hiring

It's fair to say one of the most challenging areas in business is hiring the right people. The reason I see this being challenging for most business owners is that they do not have a system for hiring or they do not follow the system they have created. It is not as simple as placing an advertisement online, sorting through some resumes, having an interview and awarding the role. A lot of thought and planning needs to go into defining the role and skills required, deciding whether the role needs to be performed locally or overseas, profiling the right people and then selecting and onboarding the person to set them up for success.

The right role

Recruitment is a key aspect of any business, and can be done using a simple process. As I mentioned, 'hire slow, fire fast'.

The 'hire slow' part does not necessarily need to take a long time; you just need to have a series of steps in your recruitment process to ensure you are ticking the right boxes. Often the reason many business owners fail to delegate effectively can be traced back to ineffective recruitment. It's possible the tasks or role weren't described accurately enough along with the needed skill set or training required.

Most business owners fall into the trap of urgency and start saying to themselves they simply 'need someone and they need them now. This person looks good, away we go!' What they don't understand is recruitment requires a system, and from the many available, only one or two will work for their business. It's exactly like time management: you have to practise over time, as practice makes perfect.

Here are the three essential steps to define the role:

1. Identify the role.

2. Define the skill set.

3. Work out your non-negotiables.

Step 1: Identify the role

First and foremost, you need to identify the role. You need to consider what tasks you're putting together and what the particular role will entail.

- What is the job title?

- Is this a local or overseas-based role?

- If overseas, which time zones will work for this role?

- What are the daily, weekly, monthly and quarterly tasks required?

The more detail you can go into, the better your chances for recruiting the right person. Write it all down.

Go to www.stopdoing.com.au to download some worksheets that will assist you in this process.

Step 2: Define the skill set

Once you identify the role or task, consider what particular skills the successful candidate will require. For example, do they need:

- any particular computer skills
- to be able to work with certain technologies
- particular training or qualifications?

Assess people against the skills you need. Don't just take their word for it—you need to include in your recruitment a way they can display their level of skill in specific areas. The way to assess this depends on the skill. You might ask them specific questions, or ask them to produce a sample of work displaying that skill. It's possible, in some scenarios, to give them a try, so you can assess their skills on the job.

For example, let's say I need somebody to have intermediate-level Infusionsoft skills. I may develop two or three questions in my interview process asking them to explain to me a process I would expect them to know, and see the feedback they give me. Alternatively, I may put together a quiz with half a dozen questions they have to answer, in order to show their competency in those areas. Finally, if I'm satisfied they have the knowledge, I may ask them to demonstrate those skills for me in the system itself.

Step 3: Work out your non-negotiables

Finally, identify any non-negotiable aspects of the role, especially if hiring overseas. One non-negotiable aspect might be their time zone. In my business we hire quite a number of people in the Philippines. Depending on the time of year, it's only two to three hours behind Sydney time, which is great because it is non-negotiable: everyone who joins my team needs to be available between 9 am and 5 pm Sydney time, especially those in general administrative support roles.

We have trialled this in the past to give people flexibility, to see if it works in these particular roles or not. If it doesn't, then we change it to suit the needs of the business. There are also other roles where the time they work is flexible, but it's important to consider each particular role and what is non-negotiable and what is negotiable. Whether it's the times they work or the credentials, experience, qualifications or skills they need, work out what is non-negotiable for you.

Employing locally or overseas

Before you jump into recruitment, you need to work out whether a local or overseas or virtual team member is going to be the right fit for your business. You might be wondering why a business would recruit someone overseas as a virtual employee. The main reason is the large cost saving involved. While in the past it's been frowned upon when a business outsources overseas, in today's global economy it's becoming more acceptable in small business.

There is an amazing pool of talent worldwide comprising highly skilled people that you can employ at a fraction of the cost of a local team member. With such a variety of talent available, you would be remiss to not consider the cost savings. It's a balance between that cost saving and the skills required for the job.

You may find employing local talent with a specific skill set is expensive because of supply and demand. Locally, there may be low supply and high demand, which drives the price of employment up, whereas if you were to look overseas, you might find there is a high supply of people with the needed skillset, which brings the price down.

In our growing economy, it's an extremely competitive market. If we can keep our costs down and make our businesses more profitable, it leads to greater success at a faster rate. We need to balance local and overseas outsourcing.

It's critically important to understand not all roles can be outsourced overseas. Specific roles may require someone local. For example, in my business, I hire a virtual assistant who resides in Australia because I want a front-line person who can speak with clients, be a client concierge and answer the phones. It was important the person recruited had outstanding English and a natural understanding of the Australian culture and business environment.

However, my personal assistant resides in the Philippines, and has worked with me for four and a half years. She speaks English well, but has never had to converse directly with clients, except through email or Skype messages. For that particular role, having my personal assistant in the

Philippines works well. However, what works for one business may not necessarily work for another; having a personal assistant residing overseas may not work so well for you.

You might be thinking, what about the benefits of having a local employee, on premises? It depends on what comes from your activity inventory and what's on your Stop Doing List. For example, I coach an accountant and part of the administrative role in his business is that the assistant goes to the bank every day, banks the cheques, goes to the mailbox, collects the mail, and does a lot more errands requiring someone to physically be in the office. These are examples of tasks that need someone local to be completed.

Another thing to consider is what works for you as an individual. Some people like face-to-face interaction, and would prefer to invest more in the right person and have them within their office. Others prefer having the value for money that comes from outsourcing overseas, so long as the task is done right.

Both have their pros and cons. Ultimately, you need to get clear on what is non-negotiable for you, and assess whether going overseas or staying local has the most benefit for your business. A few of the pitfalls arising from employing people virtually tend to be similar to those you run into when you employ locally:

- not communicating effectively and regularly enough

- not training those working for you properly, which inevitably leads to failure every time.

Whether you have people locally or offshore, it's vitally important you train them and teach them your methods.

Pitfalls specific to overseas staff include not taking into consideration time zone differentials and a lack of strong English-speaking skills. But both of these things can be prepared for through careful interviewing and clearly communicating work-hour expectations.

Essentially, it's about understanding yourself and how you run your business. If you can get someone to perform a task overseas at a fraction of the cost, by someone who speaks English and is just as capable and skilful as someone locally, why wouldn't you? It makes good business sense to keep that cash flow to increase profitability so you can invest in other areas of your business.

Finding your overseas staff

There are companies that operate more of a traditional recruitment-style service (www.staff.com or www .virtualstafffinder.com), assisting you in finding overseas staff for specific roles. These companies tend to have great processes to help you detail the job description, what skills are required, and find candidates that may fit your desired role.

Since the odds of having a negative experience with virtual assistants are, unfortunately, quite high, I'm a big fan of having the recruitment done for you. I recommend Virtual Angel Hub (www.virtualangelhub.com), which was responsible for the recruitment of my virtual team.

The team at Virtual Angel Hub have expertise in finding the right types of virtual assistants to support you. They match you with a virtual assistant they believe will be able to work well with you, and has the skills you're looking for. From there they train your assistant in how the tasks are to be done, but also train you on how to work with your virtual assistant.

There's a small fee for taking this approach but, knowing what I now know, I would not hesitate to use this service again. In the past I spent literally hundreds of hours searching for virtual staff, training and refining them. Now I've got a service that can do the majority of that for me.

The other great thing is if someone resigns or it's not working out, they find the next person for you, plug them in and away you go.

The right person

It's important through this recruitment process that the recruit matches the role, both in personality and career ambition. And it's crucial to verify what they're telling you through thorough reference checks and behaviour testing.

Personality

Personality can really make the difference in the long term. You need to ask yourself whether you can work with this person daily, knowing you will spend a good 30 to 40 hours a week with them. If you don't get a good vibe from the start, or if their personality or behaviour style doesn't fit well with the role, it's important you make a reassessment. If you fail to do this, you will find yourself unhappy with the person you have recruited and will soon be back looking for another person to hire.

Another factor many business owners don't cover during the recruitment process is assessing the potential recruit's energy levels. I try to conduct one interview in the morning and the other in the evening, as I'm interested in seeing the energy of the person at two different times of day. In a perfect scenario, my recommendation would be to have three interviews, one from a different person, so as to give an unbiased, fresh input into the recruitment of a potential team member.

If you don't have anyone else within your business, ask a friend, a trusted advisor, a coach, or someone you trust to interview this person to give you some insight.

Growth potential

You should also assess the growth potential of the role. If you think someone is overqualified, you may see them getting bored very quickly and moving on. Be sure to ask questions during the recruitment process to understand their career goals, and what they're looking to achieve. See if you are able to facilitate and support their growth; otherwise, you will lose good people fast.

References and behaviour profiling

This is often an undervalued area in recruitment, both in local and overseas hiring. We think people will only put forward references who are going to give them a glowing review. In fact, you get a lot of insight doing reference checks. An invaluable question to ask when reference checking is, 'Would you hire this person again and why?' Really make sure you ask that question, because it's extremely valuable. It's often unexpected by the person giving the reference, so you are more likely to get an honest answer. If you're using a recruitment company, they can help get through all the reference checks early on in the piece, saving you a great deal of time and hassle.

Finally, you can try behaviour or style profiling. One of the easiest methods to use is DiSC profiling. This method gives an understanding of behaviour styles and can be an easy way to identify what behaviour styles are essential for certain roles. This gives you a scientific approach to recruitment, and you aren't solely going on someone's interview responses.

Recruiting based on business culture

A key part of recruiting anyone is conducting a cultural evaluation. Have a clear understanding of the core values of your business and ensure the person you're inviting to join your company shares or displays those core values. This is where so many businesses get it wrong. They simply hire based on skill set, not taking into consideration cultural fit. In most cases, if you get the right cultural fit, you can teach people the skills. If you're tossing up between cultural fit and skills, always put cultural fit first.

This means in an interview, you're asking questions to see how they respond to your culture. For example, it could be part of your core values that you are solutions-focused. Ask them to share experiences to determine whether they're a solutions-focused type of person. Some examples are:

- Share a time, in a previous role, when you were up against a major challenge.
- What was the challenge?
- How did you overcome the challenge?

- If you were faced with this challenge again what would you do?

- If you were faced with a challenge in my business, such as a mistake on a job for a client, how would you go about resolving that issue?

I know it can be hard to work out the right questions to ask, so I have created a list of interview style questions. Simply go to www.stopdoing.com.au to download the questions.

Creating a great business culture

You need to establish your business culture as normal with your new team members, from the moment they're interviewed through to becoming a normal part of your team.

If you want to build a culture that will grow your business without your presence, you have to support risk-taking. No one wants to be micromanaged. The more independence you build in your team, the more value you build into your business for an eventual buyer, and the less time you must spend on helping solve problems.

Having a culture where staff have responsibility and authority, where people feel valued, is key to staff retention. Believe it or not, people want to be held accountable, and they want to feel in charge of something.

The next step to building a great business culture is having a solutions focus within your business. It says 'If a mistake is made, we don't dwell on the mistake. We come up with ways we can solve it and ensure it doesn't happen again.' This is a sign of a strong, growing business. When a business has a fixed mindset and business owners have fixed thinking, they don't grow.

Siimon Reynolds talks about this concept in his book *Why People Fail*. A growth mindset supports risk-taking and understands mistakes will be made, but the impact of mistakes is minimised through systems, which is critical to growing a great business.

Creating the culture from the outset is about getting buy-in from your new team member right at the start. Even during interviewing, you should be talking about your business culture, and the expectations that will be on that person to contribute to it. The onboarding process can be designed to reinforce your culture.

Role-based vs task-based hiring

You will approach hiring differently depending on whether a role is role-based (ongoing) or task-based (one-off tasks or projects).

It is really important to understand the difference between recruiting for a specific role within your business or simply on a task-only basis. It's up to you as a business owner to make the determination as to which type of outsourcing you need or want to use. Determining whether you need to hire a person for a role or just contract a person for specific tasks is quite simple. Simply refer back to your Stop Doing List and review the frequency with which you perform the task in question. The more frequent (daily, weekly or monthly) the more likely these tasks will become a role within your business. The tasks that are more ad hoc or less frequent can be assigned to someone on an as-needed basis.

Role-based recruitment

With role-based delegation, you might have different professionals doing different tasks for you. For example, role-based delegation might be hiring a bookkeeper, so they're going to consistently do your books. You could also require a senior online strategist to take care of the online aspects of your business, if you need assistance to work out Facebook, Google and other online media sources.

This might be compared to a virtual assistant who manages your calendar, diary, emails, conducts research and even books flights for you. You might also have part-time personal assistant who comes into your business, sits in the office and manages clients or phone calls. These are still role-based, but not being outsourced.

To break it down simply, role-based task delegation is recurring, whether daily, weekly and even monthly, so is ultimately a regular role in the running of your business.

If you're looking for local role-based staff, recruiters are essential in the process, as are various job board sites such as www.seek.com.au and www.jobsearch.com.au. There are countless small businesses that specialise in local recruitment, so you can look at your own network and usually find a referral quickly. If you have a database of contacts, you can send out an email to your database advising them you're looking to fill a particular role. This can turn up some great referrals for potential team members. Additionally, social media such as LinkedIn and Facebook are also becoming more and more prominent in helping find great employees.

For role-based activities, recruitment is more like the traditional recruitment many business owners are used to. It will usually involve a series of advertising and interviews, and can take a few attempts before you find the right person. This is where a recruitment business can take a lot of the hassle out of the process, as they already have the right tools and procedures in place to filter the applicants, check references, arrange interviews and perform personality tests. Don't underestimate the time you can save by only having a handful of qualified applicants to interview personally at the end of the process, instead of having to go through dozens of applicants, many of which don't fit your requirements.

Task-based recruitment

Task-based outsourcing or delegation is where you might bring in external resources for a project at a specific time, and may not use it again for quite a while.

For example, when I'm preparing for a seminar I'm hosting, I often need to create a PowerPoint presentation. I used to do this task myself, which would take hours and hours of my time. Now I simply create a mind-map for what I want each slide to have, then outsource the task to someone like Alex, who is a virtual contractor who produces my slides for me. When I set up the project with Alex, I specify exactly how many slides it needs to be and ensure the price is agreed upon. Then all Alex needs to do is create the presentation for me. Alex often turns this project around in less than 48 hours for less than $100AUD. The time I now save can go into practising the presentation and ensuring my clients receive an amazing experience. Essentially, when you begin to outsource, you may find you have people you call upon infrequently but have the skills to take care of one aspect of your business.

When it comes to task-based activities, websites such as Upwork, Fiverr and Freelancer are beneficial because you can post a job or a particular project on them. You can request specific freelancers to offer you a proposal, and you have the ability to check their work, reviews and assess them for the task.

If you are looking locally for task-based staff, try the local newspaper, local networking groups or social media (Facebook and LinkedIn have worked well for me in the past). There are many small businesses that specialise in the particular area you're trying to recruit. Remember that task-based activities are more flexible than role-based ones. As long as they meet their deadlines and meet your standards, when they do the work is far less relevant.

Task-based recruitment is different as often you're not interviewing them in person. When looking to hire a new contractor for a project, I like to view examples of their work that are of a similar style and standard to what I'm looking for, and speak to people they've done work for in the past. If you're outsourcing tasks, websites such as those mentioned earlier all have feedback mechanisms built in. Positive reviews are essential in building confidence in their ability to complete your task. Always talk to people within your inner circle and look for referrals.

Onboarding

Look at onboarding as working with a blank canvas. The onboarding process really sets the tone for the standard expected of new staff members, and integrates them into your organisation. It's often an area lacking time investment, but it's critically important.

Be prepared

Ensure everything is set up prior to the new team member starting. Don't get to their first morning without having their emails ready, or their access logins set up. You must have all those items sorted a week before they start. There's nothing worse than bringing someone in who doesn't feel you're ready for them and therefore, are just looking around for tasks to do. It's not a very good first impression.

Ensure you introduce the new team member to everybody within your existing team, so everybody can meet them and they feel welcome. This should happen regardless of whether someone is virtual, or local within your office. It can make a huge difference in the long run as to whether they succeed or not.

You should also have a training plan ready for the first six to 12 weeks for their role, and know what progress you expect them to make over that period of time. You might set week one as familiarising them with your systems and two tasks you're going to train them in. Week two could be where you train them in the next two tasks, and so forth. Many mistakes are made in onboarding when too many activities are given to the team member right from the start.

Your culture needs to be instilled in new staff members from day one. It should be easily definable, remembered and followed day to day. You need to make sure you're teaching your core values and everything else through your onboarding process. Don't just verbally explain it to them; make sure it's supported by reading material and questionnaires, along with visual elements or role-playing to reinforce it. Remember, every person learns differently. You need to cater to different learning styles to ensure your training is absorbed and remembered.

Ensure you're checking in with the core values regularly, to reinforce the importance of cultural fit into your business throughout the onboarding process.

Set expectations

When you're onboarding, you're looking for:

- *A clear understanding of the culture of your business.* Your team member needs to be brought in and have your culture defined to them. They need to understand what's expected from them from a cultural perspective within your business.

- *An understanding of the standards you expect from them.* Often these are things such as:

  - 'We expect you to start work at this time and finish at that time.'

- – 'We expect you to show up to weekly team meetings at this time.'

- – 'We expect, if you wish to request leave, you give this amount of notice.'

- – 'We expect open and honest communication at all times, which means if something is bothering you, you'll bring it up, rather than getting frustrated by it.'

- – 'We expect you to feel you can give us constructive feedback at any time.'

- *An understanding of the communication channels and expectations for your team member.* They need to have one person as a point of contact, not multiple people, otherwise you're sending the wrong message and creating confusion. Set out:

  - – Who should they go to with a problem.

  - – Who's their first point of call.

  - – What method of communication is appropriate at which time. (e.g. email vs speaking directly)

  - – Who's responsible for what, within the organisation.

  - – Who are they accountable to.

A secondary benefit of the onboarding process is it can become the confirmation of whether you made the right decision about a team member. If a team member isn't going to work out, it's generally going to be clear within the first three months, so you need to be cautious how much time you invest in this person up front. It needs to be the right amount, not too much, because if they're the wrong person, you would have wasted a lot of time. Once they've proven themselves with a couple of tasks, and they have taken on those tasks, understood them, and are performing at the standards you expect, then you have some extra confirmation, and can invest further time into them. Having good, open communication in the beginning really helps the process. Check in regularly with your new team member to ensure they're happy, and you're happy with their progress. If it's not working, or it's not a win–win situation, it's never going to work.

The balance there is in trying not to give too much to them too soon. If you invest a lot of time training them and then they leave, that's a lot of wasted time.

The next element of onboarding is ensuring you're training them in specific tasks (discussed further in chapter 8), explaining why this task is important, and what they're responsible for. Show them how to perform their duties, and then get them to repeat it back to you, so you can confirm they've heard and understand the role and the way you want it done.

Ideally, throughout training you want to have video tutorials or audio training recordings for them to watch or follow. This is important. Enable your new team member to contribute to the process if you've brought them in from somewhere else. They may have prior knowledge, or know a more efficient or effective way to do the activity you're training them in. If you don't agree with how they're suggesting you do it, you simply need to explain to them why you've chosen your way. You want to encourage contribution from your team member by listening to them and taking good suggestions on board.

Check in

Check in with your new staff member along the way. I tend to do a check-in at the end of day one and say 'How did you enjoy today?' Generally, they haven't done very much by the end of day one, but you'll both have a sense of the personalities at play.

You then want to do a review at the end of each week of their first month, and a monthly review beyond that for the first three months. (A normal probation period is between three and six months, but the standard is three.)

What you're looking for is open lines of communication. Do they feel like part of the team? Do they feel comfortable in their role? Don't just ask vague questions such as 'Are you happy?' or ' Is everything okay?' Ask specific questions such as:

- What are you liking about the role?
- What are you disliking about the role?
- Do you feel you can take more on?
- Am I training you at the speed that works well for you?
- How are you enjoying working with the other members of the team?

Check in with other members of the team as well. Are they enjoying or not enjoying working with the new staff member? What feedback do they have?

You need to be open and honest with the new recruit. If they're the wrong person and the wrong fit, you need to decide during the initial period whether you're going to move them on, or set them up for greater success.

Train them up

Over the longer term, you need to structure the team member's training based on optimising them within their role. Start with the end in mind: work out what they already know based on their prior training and initial skills, and what's really easy for them to learn. From there, you can sit down with them during the initial phases of training to work out a training program, outlining how you're going to teach them over that period of time.

Training needs to happen regularly, and should be shaped around their role or tasks. If it's something they'll be doing day in and day out, they'll gain competence quite quickly, and additional training isn't required unless you're changing the task. However, if it's something that will happen occasionally, consider tools such as checklists to help them, and check in on them regularly to ensure they're prepared. An example might be to run quarterly training in your business. You may run a short training session to keep everyone's knowledge current, leading into training for a new system. You can then run through the new training to ensure everyone is up to speed and on the same page as it gets rolled out. Refer to chapter 8 for more on training.

Moving a team member on

Sometimes a team member, for some reason, isn't the right fit, either for the role or for the business. If you feel they're the right person for the business but in the wrong role, you can move them to another available role within the business. However, if there's no role, then unfortunately, you have to move them on.

Moving a team member on without creating issues can be challenging for many business owners who lack the experience to handle the situation properly.

The good news is, if your communication has been open and you're checking in regularly with your team member, they will often choose to leave of their own accord. They'll see the role isn't right for them. However, if you have to have that conversation, make sure you keep good documentation throughout probation. Keep a record of:

- when you initially trained them in their particular task or area
- when you've pulled them up on something
- how many times you've revised and retrained them.

Keeping records such as these helps as you can go back and have a factual conversation about their lack of progress or competence for the role.

Hopefully, you'll be able to part ways peacefully, and you can take on board any feedback on the process to improve your own systems.

CONCLUSION

The Stop Doing List system will truly transform your business and your life. The key is to commit to it. Remember: commitment to your strategy is more important than the strategy itself. In order to jump-start your implementation of this system, here are two things you can do now:

1. Have your management team (and employees) read this book. This will give everyone a common context for implementation.

2. Download the tool and begin filling it out—go to www.stopdoing.com.au to download the Ultimate Stop Doing List Tool and begin work.

Remember: this system is incredibly simple and easy to use. Time is more valuable than money. Yet very few business owners think and act and make decisions that way. Make the decision to focus on your genius and stop doing everything else. It's the difference between making a living and making a fortune.

RESOURCES: WHAT TO STOP DOING

This section has been designed to give you examples of tasks that business owners I have worked with have successfully stopped doing. If they can, then so can you!

Audio & video editing

- basic video editing
- uploading files to YouTube and Vimeo
- editing audio files by removing background noise and improving volume levels
- trimming footage segments and producing rough and final cuts
- recording, editing and setting up podcasts and inserting them onto webpage
- creating and editing rudimentary graphic design tasks on Photoshop and other image editing software

Content writing

- articles
- infographics
- newsletters
- industry-related book reviews
- responding to comments made on the business's blog
- white papers
- ebooks
- designing and creating content for brochures
- how-to guides
- blog posts
- press releases
- interviewing industry sources to write an in-depth report on markets
- case studies
- preparing PowerPoint/Keynote presentations
- turning raw data into a detailed report and slideshow
- creating weekly operations reports

Customer relations

- checking email
- responding to customer inquiries
- online chat support

- creating and sending out greeting cards
- creating and sending invitations
- creating and sending newsletters
- creating and sending thank-you notes
- scheduling appointments
- receptionist duties
- answering calls
- creating forms for customer feedback
- creating online surveys for customer feedback

Financial duties

- generating invoices
- creating weekly sales reports
- bookkeeping and payroll duties
- paying bills
- transferring funds
- taking care of customer refunds
- collecting documents for tax season

General administrative tasks

- filing reports
- establishing, updating and managing a calendar of important events
- proofreading documents and other office materials
- producing graphs from spreadsheets

- checking messages
- database entry
- database updates
- performing generic errands for the office, including buying items online, arranging locations for office parties and hiring a cleaning service
- creating and managing spreadsheets
- searching for hotels, booking air fares and mapping out trip itineraries for business
- managing calendars
- setting appointments
- collecting timesheets

HR

- putting together welcome and goodbye packages for clients and staff
- placing ads on career websites, reviewing resumes and contacting the right candidates
- training on-site employees, virtual staff members or freelancers
- recruiting for potential contractors or freelancers
- preparing training manuals for new staff members or remote workers

Research

- researching important data, statistics and facts for meetings, presentations or blogs

- monitoring and reporting on latest industry developments and trends

- searching for and contacting industry experts or guests to participate in podcasts and webinars

Social media

- opening an account on Facebook

- opening an account on Twitter

- opening an account on Google+

- opening an account on Instagram

- observing competitors on social media by looking at rankings, online visibility and keyword prioritisation

- sharing relevant information

- thanking customers for mentions

- updating all social media accounts on a regular basis

- researching the important hashtags of the day and working out if any align with the company's objectives

- writing and sharing posts

- collating social media results thorough analysis on traffic, shares and mentions
- engaging with audience
- responding to inquiries
- optimising posts for SEO
- creating pinnable pictures for Pinterest
- running social media contests or challenges
- uploading photos to Flickr, Pinterest and Instagram as part of marketing strategy

Technical support

- managing spam
- organising technical support
- launching and maintaining cloud computing accounts (Dropbox, OneDrive, Google)
- converting, merging and splitting PDF files
- database building
- updating plugins
- creating a business-wide project management system online

- writing down minutes
- transcribing voicemail
- transcribing video
- transcribing audio
- transcribing podcasts
- transcribing meeting recordings
- creating documents from handwritten drafts
- creating documents from dictations

INDEX

AN INVITATION FROM MATT...

Congratulations on picking up this book. You have taken a positive step towards discovering your own personal mastery and I hope you'll find it a fulfilling journey.

The good news is, you don't have to do it alone.

While this book provides insights into my business coaching philosophy and methodology, it cannot hold you personally accountable for implementing and living what you learn.

As my business coaching clients will testify, a combination of accountability and education is key to accelerating growth and success.

Let me hold you accountable and give you the tools you need to be the best version of yourself.

Send me an email at **coach@mattmalouf.com.au** with the top three challenges facing your business today and let's create a road map to get you from where you are now, to where you want to be.

Matt Malouf

Matt Malouf
www.MattMalouf.com.au

MATT MALOUF KEYNOTE SPEAKING

Matt's presentations show business owners how to do the 'HOW' by breaking down processes so they can be implemented in any business, from any industry. Audiences can apply learnings in their own organisation the moment they walk out the door.

For more information on Matt's keynote topics visit **www.mattmalouf.com.au.**